# REVOLUTION!

## FRANCE 1789-1794

# REVOLUTION!

## FRANCE 1789-1794

BY

## SAREL EIMERL

MACMILLAN

SBN Boards: 333 12995 4

First published in the U.S.A. 1967 by Little, Brown and Company

*First published in Great Britain 1972 by*
MACMILLAN LONDON LTD
*London and Basingstoke*
*Associated companies in New York Toronto*
*Dublin Melbourne Johannesburg and Madras*

*Printed in Great Britain by*
LOWE AND BRYDONE (PRINTERS) LTD
*London*

# CONTENTS

# REVOLUTION!

## FRANCE 1789-1794

LOUIS XVI

# CHAPTER ONE

# THE REVOLT BEGINS

O N THE MORNING of May the fourth, 1789, a solemn procession wound slowly through the streets of Versailles, the home of Louis the Sixteenth of France. Three groups made up the procession. One was the clergy — the parish priests, bishops, and cardinals who represented the Church. Behind them came the nobles, in sumptuous black and gold robes with gaily colored plumes waving in their hats. And in front, dressed in sober black, marched the six hundred men who represented the common people of France.

The three groups, known as the Estates-General, had been summoned together by the King. The Estates had not met since 1614, a hundred and seventy-five years before. But Louis, the supreme and absolute ruler of France, was desperate. The government was deeply in debt and the treasury was almost empty. Neither the King nor his ministers could think of a way to raise the money needed to carry on the government. In his despair, the King had turned for help to the three Estates — the traditional representatives of the French people.

The meeting of the Estates had created enormous excitement throughout France and huge crowds lined the streets of Versailles to watch them go by. Even more than their King, the common people of France had placed their hopes in the Estates. For most of them were desperately poor. Millions could not even afford to buy bread and kept alive only by begging in the streets. But while the peasants and workingmen starved, the nobles lived in luxury. And the people were helpless because it was the King and his courtiers who controlled the government. Now, the people hoped, a change would come. The Estates would destroy the nobles' privileges, and guarantee the people a fair share of the nation's wealth.

The people were not bitter against the King himself. They took it for granted that they should be ruled by a king. Indeed they believed that he ruled by divine right — by the will of God. It was the Queen, the young and beautiful Marie Antoinette, whom they hated. For Louis was a weak and simple man, and it was the Queen and her favorites who really controlled the government.

Throughout France, and especially in Paris, the capital, vicious stories were told about the Queen. She was supposed to have many lovers. She was the "Austrian bitch," who took money from the French treasury and sent it secretly to her brother, the Emperor of Austria. She was the woman who was so spoiled by luxury that, when told that the people had no bread, she had remarked in her ignorance, "Well, let them eat cake."

These stories may not have been true. But the people were right in their belief that the Queen and her favorites were selfish, thoughtless, and arrogant. While people starved in the streets of Paris, the courtiers strolled haughtily around the huge gilded rooms of the royal palace, idling away their time flirting and gambling. They were incredibly small-

minded. The men quarreled over who should have the right to
visit the King in his bedchamber. The women argued over
who should be allowed to help the Queen dress. To satisfy as
many as possible, the Queen's clothes were passed from hand
to hand among a dozen waiting noblewomen.

The Queen and her favorites were also tremendously vain.
They spent enormous sums on clothes and jewels and even on
arranging their hair. At one period, the women wore their
hair piled up so high that they had to kneel down when riding inside their carriages. To pass the time, they gave elaborate parties and fancy-dress balls, and theatrical perform-
ances in the Queen's summer house in the gardens of Versailles. That house, with its walls painted by the finest artists
in France, had cost millions of francs. But it was the ordinary people who paid the bills — in taxes. And it was their
labor which supported the court, the noblemen in their magnificent country houses, and the great bishops and cardinals,
most of whom also belonged to the few noble families which
ruled France. No one had been able to change this situation.
Any minister who tried to cut down on the royal extrava-
gance was dismissed, for the King controlled the ministers,
and the Queen controlled the King.

Now, at last, something might be done. It was no wonder
that the people waited so eagerly for the Estates to meet. The
representatives of the people — the deputies of the Third
Estate, as they were called — were conservative, respectable
citizens. Most of them were prosperous businessmen or lawyers. They had no intention of overthrowing the King or the
government. Indeed they had no settled plans at all when
they first met at Versailles. They knew only that they were
determined to reduce the nobles' privileges and destroy the
power of the Queen and her favorites.

Almost at once a bitter struggle broke out between them and the King. There were six hundred deputies representing the Third Estate, three hundred nobles of the Second Estate, and three hundred priests of the First Estate. Some of the noblemen and priests also wanted to make changes in the government. The deputies therefore insisted that the three Estates should meet and vote together so that those who believed in change would outnumber their enemies.

The King refused. Louis was a kindly, good-natured man. He was not haughty, like his courtiers, or extravagant and frivolous, like Marie Antoinette. His main wish was to be left in peace to enjoy his favorite pleasures of eating and hunting and pottering around his palace, repairing locks and watches.

Still, he was the King and like almost all rulers in history, he wanted to retain his power. He was unsure of what the deputies of the Third Estate might do if they seized control of the Estates, and he knew that most of the nobles and the priests would take his side in any disagreement with the deputies. So Louis insisted that the three Estates should meet and vote separately, as houses, thereby guaranteeing him a majority of two to one.

As the weeks dragged by and the struggle between the King and the deputies continued, the people of France grew increasingly impatient. Riots broke out in Paris. Crowds thronged the roads which led from the capital to Versailles, twelve miles away. And every day the hall where the Third Estate held its meetings was packed with men and women clamoring for action.

Meanwhile, the deputies of the Third Estate were getting to know each other, and their resistance to the King grew steadily stronger. Early in June, they announced that they were no longer just one house of the Three Estates. Instead they had turned themselves into a National Assembly which represented the people of all France, and they invited the nobles and priests to join them. Almost at once rumors began to spread that the King intended to dismiss them and so keep the government of France in his own hands.

The King planned to address the Three Estates on the twenty-second of June. Two days before, the deputies of the Third Estate, trying to assemble, found that their meeting place had been closed; for repairs, they were told. That day it was raining hard in Versailles. Wet and uncomfortable, holding umbrellas to keep off the rain, the deputies wandered around the streets until they found an empty indoor tennis court. They crowded inside, surrounded by hundreds of visitors who swarmed in confusion around them. The deputies were excited and afraid that they would be arrested by the King. One deputy suggested that they should move to Paris where the people could protect them from the King's soldiers. The suggestion was rejected. Instead the deputies decided to swear a solemn oath: that they would never separate but would continue to meet until they had drawn up a new constitution for France.

The revolt against the King had now definitely begun. Like most revolutions, it moved slowly, without any definite plan. But as each step was taken, another inevitably followed.

On June 23, the King summoned the three Estates together. Sitting silent and attentive in their separate parts of the great hall, the deputies of the Third Estate, the nobles, and the clergy listened to the King speak from his throne. The Estates, he announced, could discuss taxes and reforms in the government. But "none of your plans or proceedings," he went on, "can become law without my approval." Then he commanded the Estates to be dismissed when he had finished his speech, and to meet later in separate houses. The threat was clear. If the deputies defied his orders and continued their attempts to bring the three houses together, the Estates would be dissolved.

When Louis left the hall, the nobles and most of the clergy followed. But the deputies of the people and a handful of priests remained in their seats, uncertain what to do. It was a nobleman, the Count de Mirabeau, who gave them the lead they wanted.

Although he was a noble by birth, Mirabeau had taken the side of the people and had been elected to the Estates as a deputy. He was a huge man with an ugly pockmarked face, enormous energy, and an extremely bad reputation. He was a gambler and a swindler. He had borrowed huge sums of money which he never paid back and had served three years in prison for running away with another man's wife. Few people really trusted him. But Mirabeau had such tremendous energy and he spoke with such passionate eloquence that he had overcome the other deputies' distrust and made himself a leader of the Third Estate.

"Who is it," he demanded, "that gives these orders and dictates these laws? It is one who ought rather to receive orders from us, to whom alone twenty-five million Frenchmen look for a happiness agreed upon, given, and received by all."

Mirabeau had hardly finished speaking when a messenger arrived from the King and ordered the deputies dismissed. "Go tell those who sent you," Mirabeau shouted, "that we shall not budge from our places here except at the point of the bayonet."

"Is that the reply," asked the messenger, "that you wish me to give to the King?"

"It is," the President of the Assembly answered, "for no one can give orders to the assembled nation."

This was open defiance and the King sent soldiers to clear the hall by force. But when the soldiers reached the doors, they were persuaded to go back. For the moment, the King gave way. "Oh, well," he exclaimed, "the devil with it — let them stay." Four days later, the nobles and the clergy took their seats with the deputies, and the whole Assembly prepared to draw up a new constitution for France. To the triumphant deputies and to the cheering crowds outside, it seemed that the King had been defeated and that the Revolution was over.

But the King had not really given way. He was making plans to fight.

If Louis had been left to himself, he might have accepted his defeat by the national Assembly. He was weak and found it hard to make decisions. He was also kindhearted and hated the thought of fighting and bloodshed. But the Queen and the courtiers at Versailles gave him no peace. They despised the deputies. They were enraged by the idea that these small-town shopkeepers and lawyers should have a voice in the government, alongside the nobles. Moreover, they were terrified of losing their privileges and their power. So, day after day, they kept on at the King, urging him to dismiss the Assembly by force and reassert his authority over France.

Louis allowed himself to be persuaded, and, toward the end of June, he began to gather troops around Versailles and Paris. Many of the French soldiers sympathized with the Revolution and had already deserted. But there were Swiss and German troops in the army who served only for pay and would obey any orders.

The King planned to use his soldiers to dissolve the Assembly. Then, if the people of Paris tried to revolt, he would order the soldiers to crush the rebellion.

The news that Louis was gathering troops was soon carried to Paris. The crops had not yet been harvested and the poor people of the city were desperate for food. They had placed their hopes in the National Assembly, and, as rumors flew around the city that the Assembly was to be dissolved, angry crowds began to gather. Their main meeting place was in front of the Palais-Royal, home of the King's cousin, the Duke of Orleans. The Duke was a selfish, ruthless and ambitious man. He hated his cousin and secretly hoped to take his place as king. With this scheme in mind, he encouraged the crowds to meet in the gardens around his palace where Louis's soldiers could not enter, and to carry on their agitation against the King.

On July 12, a particularly huge crowd collected in front of the Palace. It included people of all types. There were doctors there and lawyers and students; butchers in their leather aprons, and carpenters and tanners, and people who were without jobs and so poor that their tattered clothes hardly covered their bodies. For a while the crowd surged aimlessly to and fro. Then a young journalist named Camille Desmoulins jumped up on a table, brandishing a pistol.

"Citizens," he shouted. "I come from Versailles. This evening the Swiss and German guards are coming to slit our throats. There is no time to lose. We must get to arms."

Scared and excited, the crowd formed into a procession and began to march through the streets. A squadron of the King's German soldiers mounted on horseback tried to drive them back, and some of the Parisians were wounded. News of this "massacre" raced through the streets, and a group of

French soldiers burst out of their barracks and helped the mob to drive the German cavalrymen back.

The King could still have crushed the people of Paris. They were unarmed and already he had troops inside the city. But Louis, unwilling to shed blood, did not give his soldiers the order to fire, and, while he hesitated, the people prepared for battle. High and shrill above the noise and shouting in the streets, church bells sounded the tocsin — a signal that meant a call to arms. Barricades were hastily thrown up in the narrow, winding streets to hold back the King's soldiers. A new city government was hurriedly elected and it gave orders for a citizens' army — a National Guard — to be formed to defend the capital.

This citizen army needed guns. The mobs, now out of control, were also clamoring for arms. Cheering and shouting, they marched through the streets, pillaging armorers' shops. Then, on July the fourteenth, they broke into a government arms depot and seized thousands of muskets. Still the cry for arms continued, and early on that same morning thousands of panicky and excited men and women formed into a huge procession and surged through the streets to the Bastille.

The Bastille was a prison and a fortress. Its huge stone walls, nine feet thick and a hundred feet high, were surrounded by a moat, filled with water, seventy-five feet wide. High up in the walls, cannons pointed down over the city. From an outer courtyard, a small drawbridge led into an inner court. From there, a long drawbridge spanned the moat, leading to the massive main gate in the great defensive wall of the fortress.

To the people of Paris, the Bastille was the supreme symbol of the King's power. Hundreds of prisoners, arrested and kept without trial, were supposed to be imprisoned in its dungeons. Its cannons could have destroyed huge areas of the city. But no one actually planned to storm it, for the moat and the walls seemed to make it impregnable. The crowd which gathered in front of the Bastille merely wanted the governor, the Marquis de Launay, to remove his cannons and to give them the arms and ammunition which were supposed to be stored in the fortress.

At ten that morning, three delegates sent by the new city government entered the fortress to talk to the Governor. He received them in a friendly manner and invited them to lunch. When the delegates did not return promptly, the mob which was waiting outside thought they had been taken prisoner, and forced its way over the small drawbridge and into the inner courtyard. Unluckily, the Marquis de Launay was a nervous and excitable man and, scared by the crowds milling around the courtyard, he ordered his men to fire.

Caught helplessly in the courtyard, nearly a hundred of the attackers were killed. Then the attack began in earnest. Cannons were brought up and pointed at the main gate of the fortress. De Launay wanted to fight on but his men threatened to mutiny if he did not surrender. So de Launay offered to surrender provided that his men were spared, and he gave orders for the main drawbridge to be lowered. But the mob, maddened by the death of so many of their comrades, ignored de Launay's terms. They poured across the drawbridge into the fortress and began to massacre the defenders. De Launay himself was seized and murdered and his head, placed on the top of a pike, was carried in bloody triumph through the streets.

The battle for the Bastille is insignificant when compared to the important battles of history. But it had such a decisive effect that July the fourteenth — Bastille Day — is still celebrated as independence day in France. All that day, the Parisians waited for Louis's troops to pour into the city to revenge the fall of the fortress. But now that the people of Paris had proved they would fight to defend their city, the faint-hearted Louis was no longer sure that his soldiers could defeat them. Despite the pleas of the Queen and his courtiers, he decided to give up his plan to dissolve the National Assembly, and he withdrew the troops he had collected around Paris.

At last the Revolution seemed to be over and, at Versailles, the National Assembly settled down to draw up a new constitution. The King would be allowed to remain on his throne. But the nobles and the great church leaders would be deprived of their privileges, and the real power would be turned over to the elected representatives of the people.

So everyone believed in the days which followed the fall of the Bastille. Actually, although no one knew it then, the real Revolution had not even begun. Gradually, step by step, it was to spread until all the traditional institutions and leaders of France were destroyed. In Paris and in the other cities, the mobs, led by fanatical revolutionaries, would seize power. A reign of terror was to sweep across the country and its symbol would be the guillotine — a newly invented instrument that could cut off a man's head with a single, clean stroke. Not the King, not the National Assembly, not even the leaders of the Revolution, but the mob and the guillotine were to become the real masters of France.

Benezack.                                    T W Harland.

MARIE ANTOINETTE

# CHAPTER TWO

# KING LOUIS IS MADE PRISONER

---

THE REVOLUTION that had begun in Paris soon spread across the countryside of France. Before 1789, most of the land was owned by the nobles or by the church, and the men who actually worked the soil were practically slaves. Some, indeed, were actually slaves, owned body and soul by their masters. If they dared to disobey an order, they could be whipped or put to death. Other peasants were free men, according to the law, but in practice they were just as much under the nobles' control. They had to pay enormously high rents for the right to work their farms. If they did own their own land, they had to allow deer and other game to wander over it undisturbed and ruin the crops. The nobles wanted the game left alone to provide plenty of prey for their hunting. And when the hunts took place, the peasants had to stand helplessly by while the nobles and their ladies galloped over the fields, doing even more damage to the crops.

Why didn't the peasants protest? First of all, because they had no hope that their protests would achieve results. Suppose that a peasant sued a noble for damaging his crops. The case would come up in front of a judge who had been appointed by the noble. The judge would be afraid of losing his job; or perhaps he and the noble would be friends. In either case, the peasant could be sure of losing the case and, what was worse, would probably end up in jail himself for having had the impudence to protest.

Then why didn't the peasants band together and revolt? Because most of the nobles possessed their own private armies. Besides, the peasants knew that if a truly serious revolt broke out, the King himself would send troops to put it down and probably kill the ringleaders.

There is another point to consider. People living in democracies such as the United States are brought up to regard themselves as equal to everyone else. Some people are richer than others or have more responsible jobs. But Americans believe that — as human beings — all people possess equal rights. Before 1789, the peasants and workingmen of France simply did not have any such attitude. They regarded the nobles as vastly superior creatures. If a noble, riding along a country road, found a peasant in his way and slashed him across the face with his whip, the peasant might be badly hurt and bitterly angry. But he would not be surprised, nor would he fight back. This was partly out of fear and partly because he took it for granted that the nobles could do whatever they wished.

This state of mind had persisted in France for hundreds of years. The peasants hated their masters but were resigned to their fate. Then came the fall of the Bastille and the King's surrender to the demands of the Estates-General. Suddenly the peasants realized that it was possible to revolt against tyrannical rulers. As news of the fall of the Bastille spread across France, it inspired some of the peasants with new courage and also with a lust for revenge against the men who had so long filled them with terror.

In various parts of the country groups of peasants banded together and burst into manor houses owned by nobles or by local squires. They smashed the windows and the furniture and tore down the rich hangings. They burned the papers in which the squires kept lists of debts which the peasants owed. In a few cases, the peasants went further and burned the manor houses to the ground.

Obviously these actions showed how deeply the peasants — and the other poor people of France — hated their masters. It is important to understand that this hatred ran very strong and very deep; otherwise the later events of the French Revolution will seem completely unbelievable. But the hatred was also mixed inextricably with fear. For hundreds of years the peasants had looked on the nobles as being both cruel and invincible. So as soon as the manor houses had been attacked and burned, the peasants were immediately terrified that the nobles would come with soldiers to exact a terrible revenge.

This fear was fed by a mass of rumors. At that time brigands were a common hazard in many country districts. Anyone traveling along a country road was liable to be held up and robbed by a gang of highwaymen. Then there were many strange groups of woodcutters and charcoal burners: half-wild men and women who lived deep in the forests and were dreaded by all respectable citizens. A peasant would see a group of woodcutters or notice a band of brigands in the distance. In his fear, he would mistake them for soldiers and rush back to his village with the news: "The King's soldiers are coming." Terrified of being arrested or killed, the peasants would immediately make off to another village for safety, carrying the report that the King's soldiers were nearby. And, no doubt, as the story spread, the number of supposed soldiers kept getting exaggerated.

Meanwhile the nobles, their bailiffs, their stewards and their other servants were just as scared as the peasants. They sent couriers galloping across the countryside to warn their friends that the peasants were rising in rebellion; were burning houses and murdering their occupants.

So, throughout late June and July, a spirit of fear and revenge spread across France. Actually the rumors were fantastically exaggerated. The peasants did not really do much damage and only four nobles were killed. On their part, the nobles had not devised any plans of revenge or punishment. Still, it was clear that a new spirit of revolt was sweeping across France and that the peasants, like the workingmen of Paris, were capable of rising against their masters.

The mere fact that they were ready to do so produced astonishing results. One of the strangest things about the French Revolution is the weakness displayed by the nobles and by the King. They were supposed to be enormously powerful and, in a way, they were. Certainly they had enough troops to put down any revolt. But a man must possess a certain amount of courage to organize his soldiers and lead them against an enemy. Unluckily for them, most of the nobles — like Louis himself — were exceedingly weak men who lacked the necessary forcefulness and willpower. The result was that just as Louis had given way when the people of Paris stormed the Bastille, so did the nobles give way when they were faced by the peasants' revolt.

On the night of August fourth a remarkable scene took place in the National Assembly. It began when a young aris-

tocrat, the Vicomte de Noailles, rose and suggested that everyone, including himself and his fellow nobles, should pay his
fair share of taxes. Noailles went even further. He also suggested that the nobles should give up their special privileges,
such as the right to charge the peasants appallingly high
rents; or to go hunting over their fields; or the right to have
their own special courts, presided over by judges they appointed.

Noailles's speech set off a kind of frenzy in the National
Assembly. One after another, the nobles rose and announced that they were surrendering their ancient privileges. One cried that slavery must be abolished. Another
asserted that every citizen should have an equal right to
serve in the high posts of government that hitherto had been
reserved for members of the noble families.

So the debate continued throughout the night. Some of the
nobles were undoubtedly sincere and felt they were simply
doing what was right. Others apparently were carried away
by the general enthusiasm. Yet others were frightened that if
they did not make concessions in time, all the peasants in
France might join together in a nationwide revolt. So they
tried to save their property by offering to give up privileges
that no longer seemed very important. As one noble after another rose to surrender his ancient rights, the enthusiasm in
the chamber kept mounting until finally an agitated assistant passed a note to the President of the Assembly to say
that the nobles must have lost their minds and that the session should be brought immediately to an end.

So far as the nobles were concerned, it was too late. By the
end of that remarkable night, the whole social system of the
French countryside had been destroyed. No longer were the
peasants to be slaves — or even helpless servants — of the

nobles. In the future, every farmer was to have the right to own his own land. Everyone would pay equal taxes. And everyone accused of a crime would have an equal right to a fair trial.

Why did the old traditional system collapse so quickly and completely? The explanation is that it had been thoroughly rotten. And just as a whole wall of rotten wood will collapse under a few strokes from an axe, so did the few attacks made by the peasants bring down the whole ancient system of tyranny.

Still, important though these changes were, the Revolution was far from over. There was much left to be done, for the deputies of the National Assembly were now engaged in establishing a completely new system of government for France; very much as the American colonists did when they wrote the Constitution of the United States.

The American revolutionaries, of course, broke free of the rule of King George III and set up a President in his place. But the French deputies would not get rid of their King. For in 1789, most Frenchmen were still ardent royalists. To them, the King was almost a god and they simply could not imagine a government without him. Moreover they still trusted Louis himself. They blamed all his resistance on Marie Antoinette and her friends — especially on the Austrian aristocrats who continued to live at Versailles. The Assembly was determined to establish itself as a legislative body, like the United States Congress — with full authority to pass laws. At the same time, the deputies wanted the King and his ministers to administer the laws and run the government.

This arrangement left one vital question unanswered. Could the King veto laws he didn't approve of? Louis insisted that he must retain the full power of veto. The National Assembly could not make up its mind. October came and Louis was still hesitating over what to do about the new laws passed on the famous night of August fourth, when the nobles had surrendered so many of their ancient privileges. Should he consent to the laws the Assembly had voted? Or should he veto them?

It is not hard to imagine the arguments that must have raged in the palace at Versailles. There sat Louis, weak and indecisive, wanting to assert his power and yet anxious to avoid stirring up any more trouble that might lead to further bloodshed. Around him were Marie Antoinette and her aristocratic friends, urging him to be a real king, continually nagging him to stand firm and defy the Assembly. Louis's position was especially difficult because he loved his wife passionately and longed to have her admire him. Finally, he allowed himself to be persuaded. He summoned a regiment of loyal troops from Flanders in northern France to come to Versailles to protect the Palace from attack and, if necessary, to march into Paris and crush the rebellious Parisians.

At this point a very trivial event took place which was to have consequences of enormous importance. In response to Louis's orders, the soldiers of the Flanders regiment came to Versailles and, on October 1 the officers of the King's bodyguard gave a party to welcome their new comrades. It was a gay and spirited affair. The officers in their superb uniforms and the ladies of the Palace in their beautiful evening gowns sat around a huge table enjoying a typical royal banquet. The King and Queen were present. There was plenty of wine and, as the banquet continued, some of the officers had too much to drink. In their excitement, as they offered toasts of loyalty to their King, their resentment against the revolutionaries in Paris grew, and they trampled the national cockade underfoot.

A cockade was a flowerlike decoration which people of that time wore in their hats. The cockades were colored and every color represented some group or organization just as a pennant in the United States represents a school or a college. The colors of the national cockade were red, white and blue, mixing the red and blue of Paris with the traditional white of the French royal family. This cockade was worn by the citizen volunteers who had formed the National Guard, and the cockade itself had already become the symbol of the Revolution.

Next day, an article appeared in a Paris newspaper describing how, at the party at Versailles, the national cockade had been trampled on the floor by the King's officers. The newspaper report went even further. The officers, it was said, had donned in its place the white cockade of the French Kings, and some officers had even flourished the black cockade which was the emblem of Marie Antoinette and of her brother — the Emperor of Austria. Hearing these rumors, the people of Paris immediately assumed that Louis and Marie Antoinette were planning to smash the Revolution and reestablish their former absolute power over the government.

These reports happened to come at a particularly bad time. All that summer, the aristocrats who were afraid of what the Revolution might lead to, had been streaming out of Paris. Carrying all the money and jewels and furs they could pack into their carriages, most of them made their way over the frontier into Austria and Germany where they would be safe.

These aristocrats became known as the émigrés (emigrants), and nobody actually made much of an attempt to stop them. But their departure produced some very serious consequences in Paris. For thousands of Parisians, such as carriage-makers, jewelers, hair dressers, decorators, and domestic servants, had made their living by working for the aristocrats. Inevitably, the flight of the émigrés had thrown these people out of work and, as a result, they were desperately short of money.

There was another problem also. Like every big city, Paris got its food from the countryside. But that summer the supply of food had been seriously interrupted. Frightened by all the rumors of troop movements and attacks by brigands, many peasants had refused to take the risk of carrying their produce into Paris. Bread was especially short and the price had risen sharply. The ordinary people of Paris found that instead of being better off as a result of the Revolution, they were much worse off than they had been before.

When things go wrong, people often look for a scapegoat: for somebody they can blame. The royal family was the obvious target. Thousands of people were desperately short of food, yet out amid the splendor of the royal palace at Versailles, the King, the Queen, and their friends were still holding banquets. Banquets! In Paris, the poor remembered Marie Antoinette's famous remark: "If the people do not have bread, let them eat cake," and their anger against her grew. The women, who had always detested Marie Antoinette, were especially enraged, and on the morning of October 5, a group of them met together and set off toward the City Hall.

As they made their way through the streets, other women joined in. Most of them were among the poorest and least respectable women in the city. They were dirty and sluttish in their tattered dresses and skirts; on the whole, an ill-mannered, foul-mouthed and vicious lot. A number of men — toughs and rowdies — joined in the procession, and the

whole mob made its way to the City Hall. Breaking through
the doors, they poured inside and seized hundreds of rifles,
and all the cash in the city treasury.

Suddenly a cry arose: "To Versailles. Let us march to
Versailles." Quickly the idea spread. No one had any clear
plan of what to do at Versailles, but that did not stop the
women. Toward Versailles they turned and, on their way,
they forced other women they passed to join their ranks. By
the time it reached the outskirts of Paris, the mob had
swelled to several thousand. Some of the marchers were
armed with broomsticks, others with pitchforks or swords or
old pistols, as well as with the rifles they had stolen. Mingled
among the women, were a considerable number of men; how
many no one could tell. For, thinking that the King's soldiers
would be less likely to fire on women, many of the men disguised themselves by wrapping shawls around their heads
and donning skirts over their trousers.

Soon, rain began to fall. Drenched by the rain and wearied
by having to drag their feet through the mud, the women became steadily angrier. A few sharpened kitchen knives on the
milestones they passed, preparing to attack Marie Antoinette.

"How glad I should be," shouted one, "if I could open her
belly with this knife and tear her heart out by thrusting my
arm in up to the elbow."

Still they struggled on until, after marching for several
hours, they finally reached Versailles. There they went first
to the building where the National Assembly was in session,
and a group of the women forced their way inside.

"The people lack bread," one of them screamed out. "They
are in despair. The Assembly contains enemies of the people
who are the cause of the famine. Wicked men are giving

money to the millers to make sure they do not grind bread."

These charges were absurd. But inside the Assembly it soon became impossible for anyone to talk sense, as more and more of the women poured into the chamber. Some crowded in among the deputies on their benches. Others stripped off their wet skirts and stockings and hung them up to dry. Amid this scene of disorder, the deputies finally managed to reach a decision. They would send a delegation to the King to tell him of the shortage of food in Paris, and appeal for his help.

About a dozen of the women were selected to carry the message and they were shown into the council room of the Palace where the King was sitting. There, one of them fell at his feet, having only enough strength left to murmur, "Bread, bread," before she fainted.

Whatever his faults, and he had plenty, Louis was a kind-hearted man. The sight of the suffering women affected him deeply. In his own hand, he wrote a letter giving orders for food to be taken from the royal stores and sent immediately to Paris.

At this point, the crisis seemed to be over at Versailles. Louis's decision to have bread sent to Paris had apparently calmed the women. But while Louis was conciliating them in Versailles, more trouble was brewing in Paris: trouble which for the first time would place the King and his family in real danger of their lives.

Like other Parisians, the citizen volunteers who made up the National Guard had been outraged by the newspaper reports of the party at Versailles. They had burned with anger at the news of the "insult" to the national cockade. While the women were on their way to Versailles, members of the

Guard assembled and decided to follow the women. There, they would support the women's demand for food. What was more, they would avenge the insult to the cockade by bringing the King and Queen back to Paris where they would be under the control of the people.

Angry and argumentative, the Guardsmen swirled around the City Hall, while the church bells began to ring out the tocsin of alarm. Then General Lafayette arrived at the City Hall. This was the Lafayette who had fought in the American Revolution. His role in it had made him a hero to the revolutionaries in France and, by popular acclaim, he had been made commander of the National Guard.

It was not a bad choice. Lafayette was not a very intelligent man. But he did sincerely want his countrymen to enjoy the same kind of freedom which the Americans had fought for and won. At the same time, Lafayette respected his King and he hated the idea of Louis being brought back to Paris like a prisoner. Sitting astride his white horse, Lafayette tried to calm his men. They refused to listen. So enraged were they by Lafayette's appeals, that they threatened to hang him from a street lamp if he did not move out of their way. Lafayette was a brave man and the threat did not frighten him. But he decided to lead the Guardsmen himself to Versailles in the hope that he could save Louis from outright physical attack.

So the second procession of the day set out for Versailles. The Guardsmen marched like disciplined soldiers, in ranks of six abreast, their drums beating, and their flags flapping in the wind. Behind them, a huge and undisciplined mob of some fifteen thousand men fell into place. Some were honest workingmen who believed that the King could give them food and were determined to get it to feed their wives and children. Many, however, were ruffians and toughs who were simply glad of the chance to make trouble. With Lafayette leading the way, this unruly mixture of citizen soldiers, workingmen, and troublemakers followed the women along the muddy road to Versailles.

Meanwhile, Louis's advisers were urging him to get away from Versailles. He could climb into the royal carriage, they said, with his wife and two children, and drive off to another of his palaces, further away from Paris. There he would be safe from attack. He could then appeal to the loyal people of France to take his side against the rebellious Parisians and the troublemakers inside the National Assembly.

Louis, as usual, could not make up his mind. He hesitated —and was lost. The arrival of the soldiers and toughs from Paris ended his chances of escape. The royal carriage could not possibly make its way through the thousands of angry Parisians who swarmed around the Palace. However, the crowd, though angry, was not threatening. And Lafayette promised on his honor that no member of the royal family would be harmed.

It was now well after midnight and Louis and Marie Antoinette retired to bed. The men and women from Paris, exhausted from their long march, also settled down to sleep wherever they could find room and shelter in the buildings and stables around the Palace. Once again calm seemed to have descended over Versailles.

It was deceptive. For some of the women who had marched out from Paris were thoroughly vicious and they had not been talking idly when they spoke of killing Marie Antoinette. They hated her so bitterly that they actually did plan to kill her. Just before dawn, these women found an unguarded entrance into the Palace. Possibly there were men

B

among them, disguised as women. Whoever they were, the attackers crept into the Palace, exchanged shots with the sentries, drove them from their posts, and rushed up the stairs toward the room where Marie Antoinette was sleeping.

The firing, the sound of doors being smashed down, and the screaming threats of the women aroused the Queen. Hurriedly flinging on a few clothes, she rushed to the King's apartments and banged desperately on the locked door for entrance. From behind she could hear the women cursing and shouting as they stormed through her rooms in pursuit. But just before they could reach her, the King's door was opened and the Queen ran through to safety. Behind her, trying to fight off the attackers, two members of the King's bodyguard were killed.

In times of revolution, decisions are often forced by violence. The King had had no intention of obeying the National Guard and returning to Paris. But the attack on the Queen, like the attack on the Bastille, drove him to give up his plans to resist. Perhaps he was afraid for the safety of his wife and children. For the news of the attack on the Queen spread like wildfire around Versailles and it aroused the soldiers and toughs from Paris to a frenzy of excitement. In wild disarray, they thronged the courtyard outside the Palace, waving the tricolor cockade, and brandishing their weapons. When Louis appeared on the balcony, looking down over them, he was greeted by a storm of shouts: "To Paris. To Paris."

"Yes, my friends," said Louis. "I will come to Paris with my wife and children. I entrust my most precious possessions to my good and faithful subjects."

Fifteen years before, Louis and his bride Marie Antoinette had entered Paris together for the first time. They had driven in glory then, in a huge, gilded coach, escorted by mounted Guardsmen of the royal household, with their breastplates glittering in the sun and plumes waving gaily from their hats. Now the King and his Queen were prisoners and their return to Paris was a humiliation. At the head of the column marched two soldiers of the National Guard, holding aloft their trophies of victory: the heads of the two slain members of the King's bodyguard skewered on the ends of pikes. Behind them came more National Guardsmen, each one carrying a loaf of bread on his pike. Among them were the women. Some rode in wagons, others lounged across gun carriages; yet others marched arm in arm with workers or soldiers. Behind this confused, unruly mass, the royal carriage lumbered, surrounded by more women, many of them drunk and hurling curses at the royal couple. Then came a string of carts loaded with sacks of flour seized from the royal stores. And at the very rear, marched two more rows of National Guardsmen, escorting the disarmed men of the King's bodyguard and the soldiers who had come from Flanders to help defend their King.

As they marched, the Parisians, men and women alike, kept chanting: "Here come the baker, the baker's wife, and the baker's errand boy." Thus, with undisguised contempt, they jeered at the once all-powerful Louis of France, his wife, and his four-year-old son, the Dauphin, heir to the throne of France.

The procession reached a gate leading into Paris and there it was met by the Mayor. Coldly, he presented the King with the keys of the city, set on a gold platter. "What a wonderful day, sire," he said gravely, "on which the Parisians hold

Your Majesty and his family in their city." We are told that the Mayor spoke with sincerity but Louis could not keep himself from turning away and wiping away his tears.

The King and Queen were then taken to their new home. It was the Tuileries Palace which for hundreds of years had housed the Kings of France before the magnificent palace was built at Versailles. The Tuileries was dark, gloomy and rambling. No one there had expected the King and Queen to arrive, and no preparations had been made to receive them. All the rooms were dark, the floors were thick with dust, and the ancient furniture was all swathed in sheets.

"How ugly everything is here, Mama," said the Dauphin.

Marie Antoinette tried to comfort the frightened, bewildered little boy. "My son," she told him. "Louis the Fourteenth used to live here and he liked the place well enough. You must not be more demanding than he was."

But to her friend Count Mercy, the Austrian Ambassador, Marie Antoinette revealed her true feelings: "What has happened during the last four and twenty hours," she wrote, "seems incredible. No description of it could be exaggerated and, indeed, whatever was said would fall short of what we have seen and suffered."

Marie Antoinette had indeed suffered. The attack on her room had frightened her but she was a brave woman and had quickly recovered from her fear. It was the humiliation of being jeered at by the mob and, even worse, the knowledge of her own helplessness that really angered and tormented this proud woman. The French people still trusted their King: even the Paris mob still believed in the idea of royalty. But as she looked around at the dark, gloomy walls of the Tuileries Palace, Marie Antoinette realized that she and her husband were no longer rulers. They were prisoners, captives of the mob she hated and despised. And in their struggles to break free, Marie Antoinette and her husband Louis would soon bring on the next and much more deadly stage of the Revolution.

LAFAYETTE

# CHAPTER THREE

# THE FLIGHT TO VARENNES

---

THE NATIONAL ASSEMBLY followed the King back to Paris. There the deputies established their new meeting place in a long, narrow chamber that had once been a riding school and stood on the opposite side of the Tuileries gardens, close to the King's new home.

This shift to Paris caused many changes in the membership of the Assembly. Many of the nobles and the high officers of the church were now frightened. They had seen the mob of soldiers and women shouting and threatening the King. And that had happened at Versailles. What would happen now that they were meeting in Paris? Could they be sure that another mob would not gather and attack them? Within a few days, almost a third of the deputies decided to leave Paris. Some returned to their estates in the country where they felt safer than in the capital. Others, especially the nobles, joined in the stream of emigrants who were fleeing across the border into Belgium and Germany.

With many of the nobles and clergy gone, most of the deputies who remained were solidly middle-class. They were respectable, prosperous people: lawyers, merchants, and small landowners, the kind of people whom the French describe as bourgeois. These men tended to be conservatives and they had no wish to carry the Revolution any further. Their ambition was to provide France with a strong, solid government controlled by people like themselves. They were loyal to the King but they were also determined not to let the King's friends — the aristocrats — win back their traditional power. On the other hand, they were equally determined not to allow the government to be taken over by the peasants or by the poor workingmen of Paris.

Gradually, these comfortable, prosperous, dignified men set about reorganizing the government of France. The constitution they established was conservative. The members of the Assembly were to be elected by the people, just as Americans vote for members of Congress. But only people with a certain amount of money or property were allowed to vote, and these people would naturally tend to elect fairly prosperous deputies to represent them. The same was true of the new local governments set up by the Assembly. They, too, were likely to be dominated by the same kind of respectable, prosperous bourgeois who sat in the National Assembly.

Louis had agreed to accept the new constitution which, in fact, left him a considerable amount of power. Like the President of the United States, he appointed the ministers who were in charge of the administration. Even in the United States, the division of power between the President and Congress often leads to arguments between them, and in France, unfortunately, the division of power between the King and the Assembly was to lead to very great trouble. For Louis and Marie Antoinette had not really given up their fight. They planned to get help from the Queen's brother, the Emperor of Austria. Officially, then, Louis was pretending to cooperate with the National Assembly. But secretly, couriers were constantly galloping in disguise between Paris and the Austrian capital, carrying messages from Marie Antoinette urging her brother to march his army into France and overthrow the new government.

More trouble was to come from the émigrés, the aristocrats who had fled for safety from France. By the thousands they settled in little towns along the River Rhine, which lay just across the French border. They had carried away with them plenty of money and jewels, and they behaved in these little towns just as they had in the old days at Versailles. Their leader was the King's brother, the Count of Provence, who was possibly the most arrogant of them all. At the German town of Coblenz he held his court. Superbly dressed, with their stars and their medals and their ribbons glittering on their handsome uniforms, the émigré marquises and viscounts and barons gathered around the royal Count. They danced, they gambled, and they plotted their revenge. They would persuade the Emperor of Austria and the King of Prussia to march their armies into France and destroy the revolutionary government. Then everybody who had played any part in the Revolution would be hunted down and punished: perhaps by imprisonment, perhaps by death.

Still, on the surface, all seemed fairly peaceful in France as the months passed. The émigrés, after all, were on the other side of the frontier. Louis, biding his time, was pretending to cooperate with the National Assembly and obey the new constitution. And the great mass of the French people outside Paris believed that he was behaving with complete sincerity because they still trusted him.

On July 14, 1790, the first anniversary of the fall of the Bastille, a great celebration was held in Paris. The roads leading into the capital were filled with dense crowds of men

B*

and women streaming into town. They had come to offer thanks for the Revolution and declare their loyalty to the King. Fifteen hundred marched all the way from the province of Brittany, a hundred miles from Paris. They insisted on entering the Tuileries Palace. There, the leader laid his sword at the King's feet and all fifteen hundred swore that they would shed their last drop of blood to protect the royal family. All over France church bells rang out a peal of thankfulness while citizens by the tens of thousands took an oath of loyalty to the King. The greatest celebration of all was held in the Champ du Mars (Field of Battle), a great open space in the middle of Paris. There the people of Paris gathered to sing and to dance, to swear their loyalty, and to offer up prayers of gratitude for the benefits of the Revolution and for the peace that had followed it.

These people were completely sincere. They genuinely believed that the Revolution was over and that henceforward there would be peace. Unfortunately they were wrong. The long centuries of oppression by the aristocrats and by the high officers of the church had created an enormous amount of bitterness among too many French men and women. Beneath the calm surface, much hatred was still stirring. Nor was it all aimed at the rich. The people of the countryside were distrusted by the workingmen in the cities. The bourgeois were afraid that the poor would create more violence. And there was bitterness, too, about religion; between those who were ardent supporters of the Church and those who, in their hearts, distrusted and disliked all priests.

With all this hatred astir in France, further struggles were inevitable and, as it happened, the next crisis broke out over the issue of religion. In 1791, most Frenchmen were Roman Catholics — as they still are today — and at the time of the Revolution, the Roman Catholic Church was extremely powerful and rich. It owned perhaps a third of all the lands and buildings in France. The new government was desperately short of money. So the deputies of the National Assembly arrived at what seemed to them a brilliant idea. The government would take over all the church lands and sell them to individual buyers. With the money it received, the government would then be able to pay the expenses of running the country.

The deputies had another idea also. By ancient tradition, parish priests received their pay in a form called the tithe — which means tenth. Every person in the parish was expected to give the church one tenth of what he earned. But the priests were not appointed by the people who paid them. They were appointed by bishops who, in turn, were appointed by the Pope in Rome. Thus, the priests got their money from the people but they owed their jobs to their bishops, and their loyalty to the Pope.

Now many Frenchmen deeply resented having to pay one tenth of all they earned to the priests. They were especially resentful because they did not regard the priests as loyal Frenchmen. How, they asked, could a priest be loyal to France when, as a priest, he owed his loyalty to the Pope? This resentment lay at the root of the Assembly's second plan. The priests would no longer receive their tithe. Instead they would be paid by the government, just as civil servants are. In return for this payment, the priests would have to swear an oath to be loyal to the new revolutionary constitution. In other words, the priests would have to admit that they owed their principal loyalty not to the Pope but to the government of France.

This proposal led to a tremendous and exceedingly bitter

struggle all across France. Many priests, especially in the country districts, flatly refused to accept the Assembly's plan. They refused to put their loyalty to France ahead of their loyalty to the Church. The government, they argued, was not God. It could not give orders about religion to the Church or to the priests. To this the Assembly replied that, priest or no priest, every Frenchman must be loyal to his country and must obey all laws passed by the government.

Sunday, January 16, 1791, was the day appointed when every priest in France had to make his decision. Would he obey the Assembly? Or would he remain loyal to the traditions of the Church? The entire country was stirred by very deep emotions. Half the people were horrified by the Assembly's action, which they considered to be a sin against God. Others hated the priests because of the arrogance they often displayed, and were delighted by what the Assembly had done. They rejoiced at the thought that now the priests would have to obey a government elected by the people.

It is not hard to imagine the tension of the people who flocked to mass on that cold January morning. In Paris the priests were especially unpopular, and the city seethed with excitement. Afraid that fights would break out, the city government had ordered out the National Guard and everywhere the streets were lined with soldiers. Inside the churches, the congregations waited impatiently for the priests to announce their decisions. Churches are supposed to be quiet places of peace and love and worship, but that day few Parisians felt much love for the priests who stood before them.

As the services ended, the priests in some churches mounted the pulpit and promised to take the oath. Others flatly refused. One can get some idea of the emotions that were aroused by what happened at the Church of Saint Sulpice.

The priest who officiated there had already declared that he would refuse to take the oath, and the church was crowded to the doors with angry, hostile Parisians. Taking his place in the pulpit, the priest first delivered a passionate sermon about how all sinners would be condemned to eternal hellfire. Then he went on to attack the deputies of the National Assembly. Obviously he meant that they were sinners and would be punished by God for the laws they had passed. Enraged, the members of his congregation shouted to him to stop, and finally his voice was drowned out when the organist began to play a popular revolutionary song, called the *"Ça Ira."* The priest stepped down from the pulpit and his place was immediately taken by a local government official.

"Citizens," he shouted. "By his refusal to swear allegiance to the nation, this man has incurred dismissal from the public employment which was entrusted to him. He will soon no longer be your pastor and you will be called upon to name another more worthy of your confidence."

Louis was a devout Catholic and he deeply resented the actions the Assembly had taken against the Church. His resentment was so deep that it led him to come out openly against the Revolution he had so far pretended to support. For several months, egged on by Marie Antoinette, he had been thinking of escaping from Paris. In theory, both he and his wife were free to go wherever they pleased. But were they? Could they venture out of Paris if they wished to?

In April, 1791, Louis decided to take his family a few miles out of Paris to attend a service held by a nonjuring priest: that is, a priest who had refused to take the loyalty oath. According to the law, nonjuring priests were still free to hold services and anyone who wished to was free to attend them. But when news of the King's intended trip spread across

Paris, the people were outraged. To most Parisians, it meant only one thing. The King was in favor of the priests and against the Revolution. He was planning to escape from the capital in order to organize a counterrevoluton. Swarming into the courtyard of the Tuileries Palace, an angry crowd gathered around the royal carriage where Louis sat with his wife and children. For two hours the King sat there, determined to leave. Lafayette arrived and urged the crowd to let the King out. They refused. The Mayor of Paris tried to persuade the crowd to disperse. Still they refused to budge from the courtyard. Finally, defeated, the King and his family climbed out of their carriage and returned to their gloomy rooms.

This incident proved beyond any doubt that the King and Queen were prisoners. Louis's ministers still administered the government. He was still addressed respectfully as "Your Majesty." Yet even General Lafayette, commander of the National Guard, could not clear a way through a mob of people so that he could venture out of Paris. It must have been at this point that Louis finally decided to take the advice which Marie Antoinette had been urging on him. That proud and haughty woman had never forgotten the night when the women of Paris had stormed into her bedroom, or the humiliation of the ride back to Paris with the royal carriage surrounded by a drunken, jeering, triumphant mob. For months she had been pressing Louis to escape secretly from Paris and cross the frontier into Austria, there to put himself at the head of an army and march back into France as a real king.

Now at last Louis agreed to the plan, and the royal couple prepared to make their escape. It was, as they fully realized, not going to be easy. Day and night, soldiers of the National

Guard patrolled the Tuileries Palace, and every evening Lafayette himself came in to talk with his King — his prisoner. And suppose the royal couple did manage to get out of Paris unobserved? They would still have to travel nearly a hundred miles to reach the Austrian frontier, through country filled with ardent revolutionaries who would certainly stop the King if they recognized him.

For weeks, couriers traveled in disguise between the Tuileries and Austria, carrying secret messages and plans, and bringing back money to finance the escape. The plan was prepared with great care. To make sure that the King could cross the frontier, troops must be ready to escort him. But how were the troops to be placed in readiness without arousing suspicion? The conspirators' answer was that first the Emperor of Austria would mass troops on the French frontier as if he were preparing to invade France. That would give the local French commander, General Bouillé, who was a supporter of the King, an excuse to bring his troops together near the frontier. Thus Bouillé's soldiers would be in a position to guard the King against possible recapture and also to escort him across the frontier.

But how to reach Bouillé and his men? The obvious answer was that the royal family must travel in disguise. That, too, required careful planning and it was carried out by a Swedish nobleman, a diplomat named Count Fersen. He was a handsome, forceful and intelligent man who was prepared to risk his life to help in the escape because he was in love with Marie Antoinette. Probably she returned his love. Certainly he was a much more attractive man than her lazy, indecisive husband. It is impossible to say whether Louis knew of their feelings; in any case, he did allow Fersen to make the plans. It was Fersen who made the arrangements with General Bouillé. It was Fersen who bought and equipped a traveling carriage, called a berlin, large enough to carry the royal party. And it was Fersen who drove over the escape route, timing the length of the journey, so that all the plans with Bouillé could be synchronized to the last minute.

At first the escape was planned for the beginning of June. But it had to be postponed: the Austrian troops needed more time to move to the frontier. A new date was set. Then Marie Antoinette decided that one of her maids was a spy and would betray them. Again the escape was postponed. But at last, on the night of Monday, June 20, all was ready.

If the big, luxurious berlin were brought up close to the Tuileries, it would arouse suspicion, so Fersen left it out on the street on the opposite side of Paris. Dressed as a cab driver, he then brought an ordinary carriage round to the Tuileries.

The Palace was under heavy guard but one door happened to be left unguarded; to this day, no one knows why. Through this door, the fugitives sneaked out of the Palace. First the two royal children were taken out by their governess who was disguised as a noble Russian lady and carried a forged passport made out under the name of the Baroness de Korff. This imaginary personage was supposed to be the owner of the berlin because if she could pass as a foreigner, there would be no reason for any revolutionary to stop the royal party.

Hurrying across the courtyard, the governess and the two royal children jumped into the carriage. Immediately Fersen drove off so as not to arouse suspicion by remaining too long near the Palace. Then he returned to pick up the King's sister, Madame Elisabeth, who was dressed as a nursemaid.

Meanwhile Louis had been holding his nightly audience

with Lafayette. As soon as the General had gone, Louis dressed himself in servant's clothes and hurried out to the carriage. Then came an agonizing moment for the Queen. As she was crossing the courtyard, Lafayette rolled past in his carriage, so close that Marie Antoinette could have reached out and touched it. Just in time, she shrank back into the shadow of a doorway, out of sight. A moment later, disguised as the children's governess, she, too, was in the carriage, and Fersen was driving by a roundabout route through deserted streets to where the berlin was waiting.

It left Paris about one in the morning: one hour later than scheduled. Still, all seemed to be well. Ahead rode two noblemen, disguised as footmen, to make sure that fresh horses were waiting, as planned, at each of the posting stations. The berlin was large and heavy, and frequent changes of horses would be necessary if it was to reach the frontier in time.

In Paris, news of the royal escape became known shortly after dawn and it spread like wildfire throughout the capital. One humorist fastened a notice to a wall: "Citizens are warned that a fat man has escaped from the Tuileries. Those who find him are asked to bring him back to his lodgings. They will be given a moderate reward." But most Parisians were very far from being amused. Instead they were shocked and outraged that Louis had broken his promise to support the Revolution.

Lafayette was particularly disturbed because he, as the King's jailer, had declared only a few days before: "I will answer for the King with my head." Reluctant to admit publicly that Louis had betrayed the Revolution, Lafayette decided to pretend that the King had really been kidnapped and carried off against his wishes. To an aide-de-camp, he dictated a proclamation:

"The enemies of the Revolution having carried off the King, the bearer is charged with warning all good citizens. They are enjoined, in the name of their country in danger, to snatch him from their hands and bring him back to the bosom of the National Assembly."

Hurriedly copies of the proclamation were made and passed around to couriers who promptly jumped on their horses and set off to catch and bring back the King. But there were confusions and delays. Some of the pursuers were stopped at the city gates by guards who thought they were friends of the King and on their way to help in the escape. Not until ten hours after the berlin had left Paris did the first courier gallop out of the city in pursuit.

"They have too much start on us for us to be able to reach them," said Lafayette gloomily.

This was certainly the opinion of the King and Marie Antoinette. Their spirits rose as morning faded into afternoon and the berlin traveled steadily along the dusty roads, under the hot June sun. At one point the traces broke, and an hour was wasted before they could be repaired. Otherwise there were no accidents, and the royal family grew more and more confident as they drew closer to the small village where the first group of Bouillé's mounted soldiers were supposed to meet them.

These soldiers were under the command of a young officer, the Duc de Choiseul. Unfortunately for Louis, Choiseul was not a very intelligent man. He had been told that the berlin would arrive at half-past two in the afternoon. But half-past two came and went with no sign of the royal family. At four o'clock, when the berlin had still not arrived, Choiseul decided to draw his troops away. What was worse, he sent a messenger back to say that the escape plan must have miscarried and that the royal family would not be coming that night.

When the weary travelers arrived at the village, they did not find the welcoming troops they expected. Still, they were not discouraged. The frontier was now only a few miles away. Bouillé's soldiers must be somewhere in the neighborhood, and they decided to push on. Fifteen miles further along the road, they reached the town of Saint Ménehould and there they would still have been safe had they not suffered a stroke of sheer bad luck.

The posting master of the town was Jean Baptiste Drouet, an ardent supporter of the Revolution. That afternoon, Drouet had been away from the posting station, working in the fields. By chance he happened to return just as fresh horses were being placed in the royal carriage. Leaning out to pay for the change of horses, Louis showed his head and Drouet, glancing down at the banknote Louis gave him, observed that the picture on the note was that of the man who was leaning out of the window. With a shock of surprise, Douet realized that this man, supposed to be a servant of the noble Russian lady, was really Louis the Sixteenth, King of France.

The royal carriage rolled away, along the empty high road. Behind it, Drouet rushed with his news to the village Mayor who immediately ordered him and another man to mount their horses and gallop in pursuit. Now another stroke of remarkable ill luck overcame the royal party. The route, planned by Fersen, called for them to leave the main road which led on to the town of Verdun and to proceed instead along a side road to the village of Varennes. Drouet and his companion did not know this and would have gone on to Verdun. But on the way, they met a pair of postilions; for the horses drawing the berlin had been changed again and the postilions were returning with the old relay of horses. Drouet stopped and questioned them: "These horses have been drawing a large and luxurious traveling coach? Which way did the coach go?"

The postilions had heard the orders given to the drivers who had taken over from them. They had been told not to proceed along the main road to Verdun but to turn off toward Varennes. As soon as he heard this, Drouet pulled his horse off the road and galloped it furiously across the fields, taking a short cut to Varennes in the hope that he would arrive there before the royal carriage.

Meanwhile Louis and Marie Antoinette were gazing with growing anxiety out of the berlin's windows. By now they were deep in the territory where Bouillé's troops should have been waiting to protect them. But the countryside was empty. Where were the soldiers? The royal couple were baffled, for they did not know that the welcoming troops had been withdrawn because of the message passed back by the Duc de Choiseul.

When the berlin reached Varennes, both Louis and Marie Antoinette were exhausted by the long ride without sleep. They did not yet know that they had been recognized, but they were soon to find out. For Drouet, taking his shortcut across the fields, had reached Varennes first and aroused the local officials. As soon as the berlin lumbered into the village, it was stopped and Louis was ordered to get out. He was led into a small, shabby room over a grocer's store and there, too proud to lie, he admitted that he was indeed the King.

Still all hope was not yet lost. With fifty of his soldiers, the Duc de Choiseul happened to enter Varennes. By this time, the village street was crowded with people — all supporters of the

Revolution and determined to hold the King prisoner. Choiseul, however, managed to make his way to the King's side. It was clear to him that his troops could easily cut their way through the crowd and carry the royal family to safety, and he begged Louis to give him the order to do so.

But the King was tired and, as always, he shrank from making any decision that might cause bloodshed. While he and Choiseul argued, Marie Antoinette looked on in disgust at her husband's timidity. With every minute that passed, more and more people were flocking into the village, making escape more difficult. "If only I were King," Marie Antoinette must surely have been thinking, "I would not allow this rabble to stop us."

The King's hesitation proved fatal. The tocsin bells were rung, the entrances into and out of Varennes were closed. Aroused by the peal of church bells, more peasants swept in from the countryside, hundred upon hundred of them, all anxious to see and to hold the King prisoner. Against this mass of hostile people, Choiseul's soldiers were helpless, and he ordered them to retreat.

Meanwhile, a message had been sent back to Paris reporting that the King had been captured and asking for instructions. A few hours later, two couriers who had been sent by the National Assembly arrived in Varennes, bearing an order to bring the King back to Paris.

At half-past seven in the morning, some eight hours after they had reached Varennes, Louis, Marie Antoinette and their children set out on the long return journey back to Paris. Had the couriers taken only a little longer to arrive, the refugees would have been safe; two hours after they had left Varennes, General Bouillé clattered into the little town with a mass of soldiers behind him. Sadly he looked out along

the highway where the royal carriage had long since disappeared from view. There was no hope of overtaking it now.
Turning, the General ordered his men back to their posts
along the frontier.

The great escape had failed. Carefully planned as it was, a
succession of unlucky events and Louis's own weakness had
left him still a prisoner. Yet perhaps the escape had
been planned too elaborately. On the night Louis left
Paris, his younger brother, the Count d'Artois, had also
left the capital, together with his wife. Carrying false
passports, traveling in a small coach and arousing no suspicion, they had without difficulty crossed the frontier into
Belgium. There they joyfully celebrated their escape, while
Louis and Marie Antoinette were returning to face the grim
fate that awaited them.

Peint par F. Bonneville                    Gravé par N. F. Maviez.

BRISSOT

# CHAPTER FOUR

# THE REVOLUTION DECLARES WAR

---

THE NEWS of the King's attempted escape provoked a terrible anger among many of the French. He had betrayed the Revolution. He had promised to support the new constitution and then had treacherously tried to sneak into Austria. No one doubted that, once over the border, he planned to march back into France at the head of an army and crush the Revolution by force.

On the King's return journey, the people began to show their feelings long before the royal carriage reached Paris. At one point, crowds even tried to attack it. Brushing the guards aside, they climbed onto the shafts, on the mudguards, even into the box alongside the coachmen. Shouts of hatred rang through the air; "The bitch," they yelled at Marie Antoinette. And at Louis: "Traitor. Fat pig. Down with the King." Only with difficulty could the soldiers guarding the coach keep the crowds from actually attacking the King and his Queen.

In Paris, the scene was very different. There the return of the King was greeted as if it were a funeral. All along the route back to the Tuileries Palace, National Guardsmen lined the streets, holding their muskets reversed as soldiers do when a funeral procession passes. Behind them drummers beat out a steady funeral roll. And everywhere huge crowds filled every available space, in the streets and perched on the roofs of houses, all staring in grim and bitter silence at the traitorous King.

In a way the people's silence was more terrible than an outright attack would have been. It was the silence of utter contempt. What must Louis and Marie Antoinette have been feeling as they rode past the silent, accusing faces? Only two years before, Louis had been all-powerful, almost like a god. Simply to speak to him was one of the greatest honors any Frenchman could enjoy. Now he was a helpless prisoner; worse, a traitor, a man who had broken his word to support the Revolution.

Louis himself appeared dazed: "His look," said one observer, "was that of a drunken man."[*] For Marie Antoinette, so much prouder than her husband, the humiliation must have been almost unbearable. Somehow she managed to retain her normal expression of haughty indifference, as if nothing the people might do or say could affect her. Yet, in her heart, she must have suffered agonies. For next day, one of her ladies-in-waiting reported that overnight the Queen's gleaming dark hair had turned white from grief and humiliation.

The attempted escape and the contemptuous anger of the people completely changed the situation in France. It was now clear that Louis could not be trusted to obey the constitution. A guard, much stronger than before, was placed around him and his family. And now those who had always hated Louis and Marie Antoinette began to speak up more loudly. Louis must be dethroned. The whole idea of kingship must be destroyed. Henceforth, France must be ruled only by representatives elected by the people.

So spoke most of the people of Paris. But suppose Louis were dethroned? Who would take his place? Who would appoint ministers to run the government? There was only one possible answer: the National Assembly.

The deputies of the National Assembly, however, found themselves in an exceedingly difficult situation. These prosperous bourgeois had done very well out of the Revolution. Many had bought at cheap prices land that had been taken from the Church or from the aristocrats who had fled from France. Nor had they merely become landowners. They had also taken over the power that previously had been wielded by the nobles. They were now the masters of France and, like all people who obtain power, they were unwilling to make any changes that might cause them to lose it.

Nor did the peasants want any changes. Huge numbers of them had been given land that had been seized from the nobles. They were independent now; they were no longer slaves or servants. So far as they were concerned, the Revolution had gone far enough.

There was, however, one group of Frenchmen who had not benefited at all from the Revolution. They were the poor people of Paris. Some were artisans: carpenters or plumbers or carriage-makers. Some owned small shops. Others had been servants of the nobles. They were the people who had actually performed many of the actions that had brought about the Revolution. They had stormed the Bastille. They had marched on Versailles and brought the King back to Paris. They had formed the National Guard, the citizen army that had scared the King off from sending in his own soldiers to retake control of Paris. Yet many of these people were worse off than they had been before the Revolution. The troubles in the countryside had kept many farmers from bringing their bread and fruit and vegetables and meat into Paris, and the result was that the price of food had risen sharply. Moreover, tens of thousands of Parisians had lost their jobs because the aristocrats they worked for had fled from France. Few people had savings to carry them over difficult times, and thousands of Parisians were so desperately short of money that they could barely pay for food to keep themselves and their families alive.

These poor Parisians felt they had been betrayed. They had driven the King and his noble friends from power. Now the bourgeois had taken control of the government and they seemed to be just as selfish as the nobles. Inevitably, the hatred which the Parisians had felt towards the aristocrats began to turn against the bourgeois.

Angry and bitter, the poor citizens of Paris organized themselves into revolutionary clubs, and there they began to lay their plans to drive out the bourgeois and to seize the control of France for themselves. The most important of these clubs was the Jacobin, so named because its members met in a monastery which had once belonged to the Jacobin order of priests. The meeting place was a large, bare room with stone walls. Candles and torches lit the darkness, their lights flickering over the faces of the members as they sat around crude, wooden tables. The men were roughly dressed in jerseys and trousers, often patched to cover the holes. They called themselves *sansculottes* which means "without breeches" — those elegant silk breeches which fitted just below the knee and had traditionally been worn by nobles and courtiers.

Some of the sansculottes might be wearing the red cap of the Revolution, a woollen cap with an end piece which hung down behind like a pony tail. Or they might be wearing, pinned to their hats, the red, white, and blue rosette of the Revolution. The air was dense with tobacco smoke. Glasses of rough, red wine stood on the tables. Amid the noise and the smoke, the sansculottes listened to the words of their leaders stirring them up to take action against their new masters — the bourgeois.

The speaker might be the lawyer Georges Danton, a huge man with an ugly pockmarked face and an enormously loud voice. Or it might be Maximilien Robespierre, another lawyer, thin, prim and always neatly dressed. Or it might be Jean-Paul Marat, a horribly ugly little man, almost a dwarf, who had once been a doctor but now edited a revolutionary newspaper. Or it might be Camille Desmoulins, the talented young journalist who, two years earlier, had jumped up onto a table in a Paris boulevard and urged the crowd on to storm the Bastille.

All these men were soon to become extremely important figures in the Revolution. They were all members of the middle class — the bourgeois. Yet all were extreme revolutionaries who hated the prosperous, respectable deputies of the Assembly because of the indifference they showed to the sufferings of the poor. Although they were vastly different personalities, all four said the same things to their supporters who listened with eager attention as they drank their wine and puffed on their pipes.

"You have been betrayed. The towns and villages of France are still filled with your enemies: the aristocrats and their friends, and the priests who have refused to take the oath of loyalty. The rich men who sit in the National Assem-

bly are betraying you also. They have got what they want and they care nothing about you. They are no better than the aristocrats they have replaced. They are your enemies. They are supporters of the King, who betrayed the Revolution. As long as the King remains on his throne, the Revolution is incomplete. The King must be dethroned."

These speeches were all hostile, aggressive, destructive. The Jacobins had no policy, no program. Except one. Louis the Sixteenth of France had betrayed the Revolution and must be driven from his throne.

Thus, the members of the National Assembly found themselves caught in the middle, between two enemies. They no longer had any faith in Louis. But then Louis was now a helpless prisoner. The Jacobins, on the other hand, were free to make trouble and, with the Paris mob behind them, they could be dangerous. If the King were dethroned, so the deputies reasoned, this might only encourage the Jacobins to make greater demands. The deputies also had another reason for not wanting to dethrone the King. They had spent almost two years drawing up a constitution, and they were determined to stick by it. But the constitution called for a king and an administration headed by ministers appointed by the king.

The constitution also called for the election of a new Assembly. In the fall of 1791, the election was held, and a new Assembly was voted into existence. Almost immediately it came under the control of a fresh group of leaders. They were known as the Girondins because many of them came from a French province called the Gironde, and they were a strange, complicated mixture. On the one hand, they were ardent revolutionaries who hated and distrusted the aristocrats and the Church. But they were not extremists, like the

Jacobins. Instead, they were moderates. They represented the country districts of France and that meant they tended to agree with the bourgeois merchants and the peasants who had got what they wanted out of the Revolution and now longed for peace and law and order, and an end to violent change.

In many ways, the Girondins closely resembled the men who led the American Revolution. They were dedicated to the idea that all Frenchmen should be free and equal. They enormously admired the men who had organized the government of the United States, and they wanted to build up the same kind of government in France.

Like Washington and Jefferson and Madison, the Girondins were intelligent and well educated. But, unfortunately, they lacked one vital quality which the American patriots possessed. They were not practical. Instead, they were dreamers. They liked to think of themselves as heroes, like the great Greeks and Romans of classical times. Many of them drew their ideas from reading the classics. They loved the sound of their own voices and liked to make long, ringing speeches full of worlds like "truth" and "justice" and "liberty." This does not mean they were not sincere. They were completely sincere. One of them, Jacques Pierre Brissot, was a writer of political pamphlets who had fought against the old government in France and been imprisoned in the Bastille. Another leader, Vergniaud, was an able lawyer and a superb orator who could hold audiences spellbound with his speeches. But sincerity and fine words are not enough to run a country. Neither Brissot nor Vergniaud nor any of their colleagues had the ability to work out a practical plan of action and stick to it. They simply did not know how to run the everyday affairs of a government.

This was even more true of two other prominent Girondins: Monsieur Roland and his wife Manon — perhaps the strangest married couple ever to occupy important positions in a government. Madame Roland was a beautiful woman in her thirties whose mind from childhood had been filled with romantic ideas drawn from books. She used to read Shakespeare's plays while she was cooking her husband's dinner. She hated the aristocrats because she thought they had insulted her. She hated the royal family because she was jealous of Marie Antoinette. She was also enormously conceited. In fact, she was so vain that later, when she was sent to prison and knew she would soon die, she spent hour after hour gazing into a mirror so that she could describe her face with absolute accuracy in her memoirs.

Her husband, twenty years older than his wife, was tall and very thin; a long, angular stick of a man; a scholar who had absolutely no idea of how to get along with people and was at ease only with his books. He was intensely self-righteous and arrogant. He was always sure he was right and made it clear he thought anybody who disagreed with him was a fool. "That papa of mine," wrote his little daughter, "is always scolding me. It is so tiresome." Other people whom Roland scolded reacted just as the little girl did. Like all the other Girondins, Roland meant well. But he was an irritating, long-winded and thoroughly inefficient man. When he became a minister, his wife had to do most of the day-to-day work of giving orders and running his department. Her husband was so busy dreaming up grandiose plans that he couldn't be bothered to do his real job. Not that Madame Roland minded; she was quite sure she could do her husband's job better than he could. She frequently complained that he was always talking about himself, and this must have irritated her profoundly because she always wanted to talk about herself.

Still, the Rolands' house became a meeting place for the Girondin leaders. Every night they would meet in the sitting room to talk hour after hour of their plans and dreams for a perfect government and a perfect society in which everyone would cooperate, treat each other well, and be happy. It is rather pitiful to think of them arguing so earnestly and with such good intentions. For their dreams were quite unrealistic. The truth was that the people of France were not about to cooperate. The peasants wanted to be left alone. The prosperous lawyers and merchants wanted to hold onto the power they had seized from the nobles. And the poor people of Paris were determined to get rid of the middle class and take over the government themselves.

Still, even if the Girondins had been politicians of genius, the task of keeping France peaceful at the end of 1791 would probably have been impossible. It is hard to imagine the chaos which France had drifted into. But try to picture it. Suppose the President of the United States had just tried to flee from the country and was regarded by most of the people as a traitor. Suppose there were two groups in Congress (like the Girondins and Jacobins) who truly hated each other. Suppose the law courts had been abolished and in many places there were no judges or sheriffs. Suppose that many cities and states had no government at all. Suppose the value of the dollar kept dropping so that one couldn't be sure whether tomorrow it would be worth eighty cents or sixty cents or less. And suppose that in Washington, men were meeting and plotting to drive out the President and all members of Congress who disagreed with them, and then to take over the government themselves.

c

That would be bad enough. But France was even worse off. The whole country was filled with hatred and with fear.

There was, to begin with, the religious problem. Instead of getting better, it had grown steadily worse. Actually, the situation was quite simple. Some priests were prepared to take the oath of loyalty to the new government. Others were not. Yet, from this simple disagreement, the most violent passions erupted. When people's passions are sufficiently aroused, they stop behaving reasonably. They distort, they exaggerate, they lie, and they hate, and this is exactly what had happened in France.

Supporters of the Revolution looked on the nonjuring priests as enemies. They were distrusted and despised as "Friends of the aristocrats," and they were hunted down, beaten, driven into hiding, and, sometimes, murdered. On the other hand, many good Catholics looked on the priests who had taken the oath as traitors to the Church. The result was that squabbles and fights kept breaking out. In one small town, for example, a nonjuring priest went into the church to hold the Sunday service. The good revolutionaries of the town, as they considered themselves, drove him out of the church with a hail of stones. Then a priest who had taken the oath appeared in the church instead. This time it was the good Catholics who drove him out of the church. Neither side would give way, so no service was held at all. This scene was repeated all over France.

Meanwhile, the Jacobin leaders were hard at work stirring up trouble in Paris. Their main weapon was fear. The émigré nobles, they warned their supporters, were about to return to France. The armies of Austria and Pussia would march with them and crush any resistance. Worst of all, said the Jacobins, the invaders would be helped by the enemies of the Revolution who were still at large all over France. And who were these enemies of the Revolution? They were the aristocrats and the priests: all plotting, all intriguing, all preparing to strike when the time came and take their revenge on everyone who had helped bring about the Revolution.

In fact, many aristocrats had remained in France and many still occupied important positions in the government. They had been left alone for a very good reason. There were not enough revolutionaries who had the education and training needed to perform their jobs. However, this kind of practical consideration did not stop the Jacobins — or the Girondins. They, too, distrusted the aristocrats, so the aristocrats had to go.

In March of 1792, the Girondins, with Brissot at their head, took over most of the government ministries, and promptly set about discharging aristocrats by the thousand. They dismissed them from the diplomatic corps, and from the army, and from other branches of the government and replaced them with their own supporters, many of whom were completely incompetent.

Despite all these dismissals, an atmosphere of fear continued to hang over Paris. So the Girondins took another step. They passed a decree stating that all émigrés who refused to return to France would be liable to sentence of death for treason. Then they passed another decree stating that all priests who refused to take the oath of loyalty should be treated as suspected enemies of Revolution and could be clapped into prison.

According to the revolutionary constitution, Louis was still the legal head of the government. He had to sign the decrees before they could become law. But Louis refused to sign them, and this refusal absolutely infuriated the Girondins. It is easy to imagine them, gathered in Madame Roland's sitting room, arguing over what to do. The Revolution was supposed to have solved everything, but somehow it didn't seem to have solved much at all. In towns and villages all over France, the local governments were in a state of chaos. New law courts had not yet been established. Criminals were going unpunished. There seemed to be less food available than ever. Prices kept rising. The Paris mob was growing angrier. And everywhere in France, the bitter struggle over religion continued to rage.

Being the kind of people who are always convinced that they are right, the Girondins did not blame themselves for not being able to get France organized properly. Instead, they blamed everybody else. They were telling people what to do but nobody would listen. The farmers wouldn't bring their food to the towns. Priests wouldn't take the oath. The King wouldn't sign their decrees. The Jacobins wouldn't keep quiet.

Confronted, as they saw it, with all this stupidity and inefficiency and selfishness, the Girondins were almost at their wits' end. Finally, in the spring of 1792, their leader, Brissot, came up with what looked to the Girondins like a wonderful idea. They would declare war against Austria. Then the people of France, united in war against a common enemy, would start working together.

"We shall see discipline reestablished," declared one Girondin, "under the breath of battle. Hidden treason will be forced to cast away its mask." And to this, another Girondin added: "The people desire war. We shall decree the liberty of the whole world."

The Assembly was carried away in an outburst of patriotic fervor. France was surrounded with enemies abroad; rotten with treason at home. War would end all that. Together the people would rally and destroy their enemies. As the debate neared its end, a Girondin deputy rushed to the rostrum, and shouted: "We must declare war against kings, and peace with all peoples."

This is the kind of thing that is always said when one government declares war against another. It always pretends that it is attacking the evil rulers and not the people of the enemy nation. But in the France of spring 1792, the Girondins' motto was particularly suitable. "A war against kings!" It was a superb rallying cry. This would not be a war of aggression, fought by one selfish ruler against another, as all previous wars had been. Instead it would be a war to spread the Revolution. It would bring equality, liberty and fraternity to all the other poor, downtrodden people who suffered, as the French had, under the rule of evil and selfish kings and emperors.

Louis agreed with the plan. For he was tired and fed-up. As much as he could hate anybody — and Louis was not the kind of man who hates easily — he hated the Girondins, the Jacobins, and the émigré nobles alike. All of them, so far as he could see, were after their own ends. All of them were intriguing for power. None of them cared in the least about him or his wife or his children. Even his own brother was probably hoping to take his place as king. It seemed to Louis that none of these people, endlessly quarreling and threatening, cared for the ordinary people of France. If the deputies wanted war, let them have it.

That was Louis's attitude. As for Marie Antoinette, she was positively delighted. Ever since she had been dragged back in shame from Varennes, she had been writing secretly to her brother, the Emperor of Austria, and to her old friends among the émigrés. Continually, she had beseeched them to combine together and march into France. The Emperor had held back, refusing to use his own army to help her. "It is true," he said, "that I have a sister in France. But France is not my sister." But now the Girondins — the revolutionaries themselves — had forced war on the Emperor, and with all her heart, Marie Antoinette hoped that the Emperor would crush them.

So began one of the strangest wars in history. The Girondins hoped it would unite all France behind their revolutionary leadership, and even dreamed of carrying their Revolution into other lands. Louis and Marie Antoinette hoped the war would bring the Revolution to an end and put them back on the throne of France. No one even suspected that the real result of the war would be to plunge France into a ghastly bath of blood and sweep almost all its leaders to the guillotine.

SANTERRE

# CHAPTER FIVE

# THE DETHRONEMENT OF THE KING

I N THE EIGHTEENTH CENTURY almost every country in Europe was ruled by either an emperor or a king who had absolute command over his people. Most of these rulers were rivals and they spent much of their time making war on each other. However, the French battle cry "a war against kings" filled them all with the same fear. The French had proved that a people could rise up against their ruler. As long as they had confined their Revolution to France, the rulers of Austria and Prussia had not wanted to interfere. But now the French revolutionaries were appealing to all the peoples of Western Europe to follow their lead. They were dangerous; they had to be crushed. So the Emperor of Austria and the King of Prussia decided to forget their rivalry and fight as allies to destroy their common enemy.

They were joined by the French émigré nobles, delighted that their dream of reentering France in triumph was now about to be realized. It never occurred to the Austrians or the Prussians or the émigrés that they might have trouble crushing the revolutionary armies. The émigrés in particular were looking forward eagerly to an easy victory and a triumphant revenge. "I know the road to Paris," exclaimed one

c*

émigré confidently. "I'll guide the foreign armies thither, and not one stone of that proud capital shall be left upon another."

The French were equally confident. This is the situation at the beginning of practically every war that ever breaks out. Both sides usually assume they will be victorious, since, if either side thought it would be defeated, it would obviously try to keep the peace. Confident of victory, the French decided to open the war by marching into Belgium, which was then ruled by the Austrians.

The French army advanced in two columns. One was led by a general called Dillon, the other by the Duc de Biron. He, of course, was an aristocrat. Why then was he still in command of an army which served a government ruled by men who hated and feared aristocrats? The answer is that before the Revolution almost all the nine thousand officers of the French army had come from noble families. Since the Revolution had begun, about six thousand of those officers had left the army. Many had resigned. Others had been dismissed by the Girondin ministers. But several thousand had remained because there were not enough nonaristocrats available who were competent to take their place, especially in the higher ranks.

An army which has lost two out of every three experienced officers is not likely to be very efficient. In fact, the French army was in terrible shape. The politicians in Paris had been so busy fighting among themselves that they had let the army go to pieces. The troops were short of guns and ammunition, and even of boots fit to march in. Worst of all, the soldiers did not like the idea of taking orders from their officers. After all, they thought, the main principle of the Revolution was that all men are equal; and, if all men are equal, then no man has the right to give orders to another. Besides, many of the officers were aristocrats, and most Frenchmen had become so used to hearing that all aristocrats were traitors that they simply did not trust the men who were leading them into battle.

So it was with mistrust and hostility toward their officers that the soldiers under General Dillon advanced into Belgium. All went well until they came up against a line of Austrian hussars. But as soon as the Austrians opened fire, the French soldiers panicked. They simply fell into confusion, turned, and fled for their lives. Desperately, Dillon threw himself in front of his fleeing troops, shouting to them to stop their retreat. Their response was to cut him down with their sabers. No real fighting had taken place; General Dillon, killed by his own men, was almost the only French casualty. Nonetheless, in a state of hopeless confusion, the French soldiers streamed back to the frontier.

The other French column was equally terrified, and equally mutinous. One story tells how the commanding general, the Duc de Biron, ordered a group of his men to make a bayonet charge against the enemy. Two of the soldiers turned to their comrades and said: "Let us vote on the general's proposal." The vote went against de Biron and he had to withdraw his order.

When his men came up against the main body of the Austrian army, de Biron decided that he could not win a battle against the well-disciplined Austrian lines that confronted him. He therefore ordered a retreat. Instantly, a cry went up among the French soldiers: "We are betrayed."

Betrayed by what? By whom? No one knew, no one asked, no one tried to explain. The French had simply heard so many rumors of treason that they could not think clearly.

Perhaps they were also frightened by the sight of the Austrians. Not a shot had been fired, yet the French, instead of carrying out an orderly retreat, simply turned and fled. Many threw down their muskets so they could run more easily. Terrified, and in complete disorder, they stumbled back across the fields towards the French frontier while the Austrians gazed after them with astonishment and contempt.

"We do not need swords," one Austrian officer remarked, "to put the French to flight. All we need is whips."

The news of these defeats was quickly carried back to Paris, together with the cry that had now become so common : "We have been betrayed." Naturally the Girondins did not blame themselves for having started the war. Nor did they blame the defeats on the shortage of guns and ammunition. Or on their own stupidity in dismissing so many experienced officers. Or on the soldiers who had disobeyed orders and run in panic from the enemy. Instead they placed the blame on traitors behind the lines; on those mysterious traitors who were always supposed to be responsible for everything that went wrong. The army had been defeated. And who was to blame? Why, the nobles of course, and their friends, and the priests who had refused to take the oath of loyalty. They were the people who were always stirring up trouble and keeping the country in chaos. And, finally, the Girondins blamed the King.

The poor people of Paris, the sansculottes, felt much the same, except that they also blamed the Girondins. For several months the Paris mob had been fairly quiet, but now the news of the French defeats stirred them to action. In the various sections of Paris, especially in the poorer parts of the city, leaders started to call their followers together. From all sides, Parisians flocked to the City Hall. Some were respectable workingmen and their womenfolk. Others were soldiers. But the great mass of the mob was made up, as usual, of toughs and hoodlums glad of yet another chance to make trouble.

From the City Hall, the mob marched into the old riding school where the Assembly was in session. Ignoring the deputies, the mob trampled through the chamber, shouting: "Long live the patriots," and "Down with the veto." A few men held up in mockery that well-known symbol of the old regime: a pair of culottes, the breeches worn by gentlemen. Another man waved a heart, still dripping blood, that had been cut out of a calf and was supposed to represent the heart of an aristocrat.

At first the mob was fairly good tempered. The people sang and danced to the tune of the revolutionary song, the *"Ça Ira."* Marching to the Jacobin club, they planted a tree representing liberty in the garden. But when a large number of people gather together, they can easily be gripped by a fever which stirs them to violent action. So it happened on that afternoon of June 20, 1792. As they kept on dancing and singing and parading around the streets, the crowd's desire grew for some target on which it could vent its anger at the army's defeats. And the natural target, as always, was the King.

The leader of the mob was Antoine Joseph Santerre, a manufacturer of beer who had become very popular among the sansculottes because he was always ready to let them have free beer at such times of excitement. With Santerre at their head, the mob made for the Tuileries Palace. The palace was guarded by soldiers, but they had not been given any orders to fire, so the mob was able to force its way inside the palace grounds and to smash down the doors leading to the royal apartments.

In one chamber, Marie Antoinette and Elisabeth, the King's sister, were standing. Into it, a crowd pushed its way, jeering and shouting insults. While Marie Antoinette and her sister-in-law took refuge behind a table, Santerre waved his arms at them contemptuously, talking about them as if they were freaks he was showing off at a circus while the crowd behind him roared with laughter.

In the chamber where Louis was waiting, the disorder was even more violent. Louis, protected by a handful of guards, was forced into a corner while the sansculottes jeered at him, using the names they had so often used before: "Traitor. Intriguer. Fat pig." Their leader was a butcher, a hefty bully of a man named Legendre, and he delivered a loud, blustering speech in which he blamed Louis for all the troubles that had befallen France. Humiliating as his position was, Louis managed to retain his dignity. Quietly he replied that he stood by his rights under the revolutionary constitution. Someone forced the revolutionary red cap of liberty on his head, and Louis, making no effort to resist, calmly responded by picking up a glass and drinking a toast to the health of his people.

Eventually, the mob broke up and streamed away from the Palace. Once again Louis and Marie Antoinette had survived. Still, they might easily have been murdered and everyone knew it. The Paris mob had shown its power more threateningly than ever before. The people had marched through the Assembly chamber and stormed into the Tuileries Palace, and no one had been able to stop them. Who then was now in control of France? Certainly not the King. Perhaps the Assembly, led by the Girondins. Or had the Revolution now reached the point where the legally elected leaders of the government could be bullied and ruled by a disorderly gang of hoodlums gathered together from the slums of Paris?

The Girondins and their supporters in the Assembly had been especially disturbed by this latest outbreak by the Paris mob. They were the elected representatives of the people. They believed that a majority of Frenchmen supported them, and probably they were right. After all, the Girondins were responsible and respectable men. They believed passionately that all men should treat each other as equals. But they also believed in law and order: that a man should be allowed to keep the money he had worked for and have his property protected by the government.

But suppose the Paris mob, led by the Jacobins, should seize power? Then all such rights might be destroyed. No one would be safe against any group of toughs who might take a dislike to him and destroy his store, or his house, or any of his possessions. It was true that the Paris mob made up only a tiny fraction of the French population. But in Paris only the National Guard, the citizens' army, was available to preserve order, and the Guard was under the control of the city government of Paris. There was a clear danger that the Jacobins might manage to seize control of the city government. And, as the National Assembly met in Paris, the Jacobins might then be able to impose their will by force on the Assembly too, and thus win control over the legal government of France.

In fact, the struggle between the Jacobins and the Girondins was turning into a struggle between the people of Paris on one hand, and the rest of France on the other. At this point, the story of the Revolution becomes extremely confused. Today most orders and decisions given and taken by government leaders are written down. So, by studying the documents, historians can get a fairly clear idea of who was trying to do what. But during the French Revolution, most decisions were made in conversation and were not recorded in writing. There is no way to know how and why many important events occurred.

It is known, however, that sometime in June, the Girondins decided to summon large numbers of volunteer soldiers from the provinces of France. Some were to go to the front to fight against the Austrians and the Prussians. Others were summoned to Paris. Probably the Girondins intended to use these soldiers to dethrone the King. For although the Girondins had served as the King's ministers, they had never really trusted him, and the defeats suffered by the French army had led to an open break. The King, blaming the defeats on the Girondins, had dismissed them from their positions as ministers and appointed friends of his own in their place. In reply, the Girondins decided to get rid of the King altogether.

No doubt the Girondins also assumed that soldiers from the provinces would be loyal to the Assembly — which was the legal government of France. Therefore they could be used to crush any further outbreaks by the Paris mob that might be organized by the Jacobins.

Among the soldiers from the provinces, there was a body of five or six hundred men who came from the port city of Marseilles, and these men were now to play a decisive role in the next stage of the Revolution. According to a popular tradition, they were gay and romantic lovers of liberty, dedicated to the cause of the Revolution and ready to die for it. Many stories have been told about them; of how they marched hundreds of miles through the countryside, their clothes and boots falling to tatters as they went. And, as they marched, they are supposed to have sung over and over the words of perhaps the most stirring military song ever written, the *"Marseillaise,"* which was to become the great rallying song of the Revolution and is now, nearly two hundred years later, the national anthem of France.

Actually, this romantic picture of the men from Marseilles as liberty-loving heroes is quite untrue. They were not patriots. They were brigands and cutthroats who would serve anyone who paid them. Most of them were not even Frenchmen, but had been collected from the slums of Genoa and Corsica and Greece. By summoning these men to Paris, the Girondins had made a terrible mistake. For, as they entered Paris, the men from Marseilles were greeted by Jacobins who led them immediately to the workingmen's quarter of the city where extreme revolutionaries were in control. There, the soldiers were given all the wine they could drink. Drunken, lusting for a fight, and not caring who they killed as long as they could kill somebody, they were easily persuaded to join in an attack which the Jacobins were planning against the King.

The men from Marseilles had entered Paris on August ninth. On that night, the city seethed with confusion. The strongest force in Paris, the National Guard, was controlled by the city government which was called the Commune. But who controlled the Commune? Legally, the Commune, which met at the City Hall, consisted of deputies elected by the people of Paris. These deputies represented all the people of Paris, not just the sansculottes, and most of them were moderate revolutionaries who sided with the Girondins. But on the night of August ninth, the Jacobins decided on a very bold stroke. A group of their leaders gathered and declared that a revolution had taken place inside the city. As a result of the revolution, said the Jacobins, they had become the real representatives of the people.

This gang of Jacobin extremists called themselves the Insurrectionary Commune, and their claim to represent the people of Paris produced a situation of total confusion. Inside one chamber of the City Hall, the legally elected members of the Commune were meeting. In another chamber, the self-appointed members of the Insurrectionary Commune were holding another meeting. Both claimed to be the real government of Paris. Meanwhile, out in the streets, the Jacobins were using their influence over the mob to terrorize the legally elected Commune. Church bells rang the alarm, and in response to the call, thousands of men and women poured into the streets. Brandishing weapons, they raged through Paris, smashing windows, and creating a general atmosphere of fear. And in the taverns of the Paris slums, the drunken soldiers from Marseilles were threatening to murder anyone who opposed them.

These terroristic tactics were completely successful. Fearful that they would be attacked by the mobs, the members of the legally elected Commune surrendered their power. At dawn on the morning of August 10, the Insurrectionary Commune took over control of the city government. This meant they controlled the National Guard. Now, for the first time, the Jacobins had an organized body of troops under their command.

The Jacobins' first aim was to destroy the monarchy, and by force. The Girondins also wanted to get rid of the King, but they wanted to do so peacefully. If the Jacobins could destroy the monarchy by force it would prove that they were the strongest group in Paris.

By this time, Louis himself had really become a pawn in

the struggle between the moderate revolutionaries, the Girondins, and the extreme revolutionaries, the Jacobins. But Louis and the men around him did not think of themselves as pawns. The invasion by the mob a month before had alerted them to their danger and, in the weeks since, they had made careful preparations to defend the Tuileries Palace against any future attacks. Actually the King's position was quite strong. He had at his disposal a thousand men of his own personal bodyguard: professional Swiss troops who were well trained and completely loyal to him. In addition, over one thousand aristocrats were still in Paris, and they had gathered at the Tuileries, determined to die if necessary to protect their King. Finally, there were about two thousand men of the National Guard who were stationed at the Palace and were under orders to defend it against attack.

The National Guardsmen were commanded by an extremely competent and energetic officer, General Mandat. Determined to carry out his orders to defend the Palace, he had organized his men into a thoroughly efficient fighting force. But early on the morning of August 10, Mandat was summoned to the City Hall. He did not know that the Insurrectionary Commune had seized power and had summoned him as a ruse, to get him out of the way. Though reluctant to leave his post, Mandat felt obliged to obey the order from his official superiors, and he went, as instructed, to the City Hall. There he was seized and murdered.

In his place, the Commune appointed as commander of the National Guard the beer manufacturer, Santerre, who had led the mob against the Palace a few weeks before. Thus the very man appointed to protect the King was one of his worst enemies.

Shortly after the murder of Mandat, Louis awoke. By now

the whole Palace was ablaze with rumors that an attack was coming. Santerre had not yet arrived, and the men of the National Guard were summoned to parade in the Palace courtyard so that the King could inspect them. This was really Louis's last chance. The citizen soldiers of the National Guard had not yet made up their minds whom they supported. Some were still loyal to the revolutionary constitution, which called for Louis to remain King. Some were wavering, almost but not quite ready to take sides with the Jacobins. If Louis had been a stronger man, an inspiring leader, he might still have been able to appeal to the guardsmen's sense of loyalty. He might have persuaded them to defend the constitution against any attack from the Paris mob. A natural leader like George Washington or Napoleon could have addressed the soldiers and filled them with a fervent determination to fight for him to the end. But poor, plump, indecisive Louis lacked the ability to inspire anybody. He had slept badly and dressed hurriedly. His artificial curls lay flat and awkward on his head, and all the powder had fallen to one side. Slowly, heavily, the sleep still bleary in his face, he made his way down the line of guardsmen, repeating over and over again: "I love the National Guard." It was all he could think of to say.

"I see him yet," one of the guards wrote later. "Silent, careworn, with his swaying gait, seeming to say, 'All is lost.'" Behind him, the guardsmen began to mutter, even to abuse him with the familiar words: "Down with the King. Down with the fat pig."

From an upper window, Marie Antoinette had watched her husband and had understood the full significance of his failure. As he turned to go back into the Palace, she murmured to herself the same words that the guardsman was later to write: "All is lost."

And already, as the Queen spoke, the attack on the Palace had begun. From guns wheeled up to position only a few yards away, cannonballs thudded against the gates that guarded the courtyard. Over the walls, the men from Marseilles were climbing like cats, knives in their teeth and muskets in their hands. Dropping down into the courtyard, they called on their "fellow citizens" in the National Guard to turn their guns against the tyrant — Louis the Sixteenth. The guardsmen hesitated. Some tried to repel the invaders, but without much spirit. Some threw down their muskets. The rest simply abandoned their posts and went over to the enemy.

Inside the Palace, there was complete indecision. Louis, as usual, could not make up his mind what to do. Marie Antoinette was urging him to stand firm. But with them there was a city official named Roederer who took it upon himself to persuade Louis that he should abandon all efforts at resistance. Roederer was not a Jacobin. Probably he was simply a weak man who had lost his nerve. Fervently, he urged the King to leave the Palace and, with the rest of his family, to walk across the Tuileries gardens to the chamber where the National Assembly was in session, and there to take refuge.

Marie Antoinette refused to go. "You know," she said, "we have a defense force here."

"Madame," Roederer replied, "all Paris is on the march." And to the King: "Time presses, sire. There is only one thing to do and that is to ask your leave to take you with us to the Assembly."

The King stared fixedly at him for some moments. Then,

turning to the Queen, he said with a sigh: "Let us be going."

"Monsieur Roederer," asked Elisabeth, the King's sister, "will you answer for the life of the King?"

"Yes, madame," came the reply. "With my own."

So, relying on this feeble promise, Louis gave up his last chance to preserve his authority as King. Accompanied by his wife, his sister, and his children, he walked slowly across the Tuileries garden. By abandoning the Palace, and turning for refuge to the Assembly, he was in effect admitting that he had surrendered his claims to any kind of independence. Surely his mind must have been filled with thoughts of his past glory and with shame that he had to beg for safety from his enemies, the Girondins. But if any such thoughts were in his mind, he made no mention of them. The leaves were falling from the trees in the garden, and the royal gardeners had brushed them into piles to be burned. "What a lot of leaves," was Louis's comment. "They have begun to fall very early this year."

Actually, Louis need not have abandoned the Palace, for the situation there was very far from hopeless. By this time, Santerre had arrived, and under his orders the men of the National Guard had all joined with the men from Marseilles in the attack. However the Swiss guards and the King's aristocratic friends were standing firm. Not knowing that the King had abandoned them, they were still resolutely defending their positions. They had been driven out of the courtyard and into the Palace itself, where they had taken up new positions by the windows. Firing down onto the courtyard, they cut down the attackers by the score.

Held back from reaching the palace doors by the murderous fire, the attackers in the courtyard began to waver. Inside the Palace, the spirits of the King's supporters rose. It looked as if Louis could still be saved. But once again Louis's weakness was to let down the very men who were trying to save him. Over in the Assembly chamber, where he had taken refuge, he heard the sounds of the crackling muskets and, horrified as always by the thought of violence, he hurriedly scribbled out a message: "The King orders the Swiss to lay down their arms at once and return to their barracks."

Loyal to the end, the Swiss guards promptly obeyed the order. By doing so, they sentenced themselves to death. As soon as the firing from the palace windows stopped, the soldiers from Marseilles rushed inside. Vicious, drunken, and crazy to avenge the deaths of their stricken comrades, they proceeded to slaughter the helpless Swiss together with the aristocrats who had also laid down their guns. Some were massacred at their posts. Others fled down into the Tuileries gardens, with the Marseillaise in hot pursuit, and were cut down among the trees. Altogether about eight hundred of the King's defenders were butchered. The rest escaped, only to be hounded down among the streets of Paris and carried off to prison to await certain death simply because they had obeyed their orders and done their duty: to defend the King.

Louis had ordered his men to lay down their arms in order to prevent bloodshed. He received no thanks for it, even from the enemies whose lives he had saved. Like many another weak ruler throughout history, Louis was soon to find that men whose chief aim is to seize power do not care about justice or fair play. If Louis had delivered himself into their hands, so much the worse for him. That was the attitude of the Jacobins.

For several days an argument raged over what was to be done with the King. Meanwhile he was kept locked up with his wife and children in tiny cells inside a convent that had been converted into a temporary prison. From these cells a corridor led to an outside door which consisted of an iron grille. There, crowds of people gathered, and whenever the King or Marie Antoinette came into sight, they were greeted with cries of hatred and threats of death. The very sight of them seemed to rouse the mob to a state of animal fury. "Every time I looked at the grille," wrote one observer, "I thought I was in a menagerie watching the fury of the wild beasts when someone approaches the bars."

The Girondins and their supporters in the Assembly wanted Louis to be dethroned. Still, they were reluctant to alter the constitution. As it called for a king to serve as the legal head of the government, they suggested that Louis's young son should be declared King. Nor did the Girondins want to be cruel to Louis himself. They had, after all, once served as his ministers and they planned to allow him and Marie Antoinette to live out their lives in comfort.

But the Jacobins of the Commune claimed Louis as their prisoner and the Commune controlled the troops in Paris. Though it was still the official government of France, the Assembly had to give way. Two days after he had ordered his gallant defenders to surrender, Louis, his wife and his children were led off to the Temple, a prison as grim as the Bastille. There, like common prisoners serving a jail sentence, they were kept under close guard by sansculottes jailers who hated them. . . .

A little more than two years had passed since the Paris mob had stormed the Bastille. Now the monarchy too had fallen. The Revolution had destroyed its own constitution. The main question that remained was: could it save itself from the Prussian invaders who, day by day, were pressing on toward Paris?

MARAT

# CHAPTER SIX

# MASSACRE IN THE PRISONS

THE PEOPLE of Paris were overjoyed by the downfall of the "tyrant," Louis the Sixteenth. On the day which followed the attack on the Palace, the streets and houses of the capital were gay with ribbons of red and white and blue. Patriotic rosettes of the same colors sprouted like flowers all over the walls of the City Hall. In the beer houses, the sanculottes and their women celebrated their triumph with wild, drunken dances to the strains of their favorite revolutionary march, the *"Ça Ira."*

In long lines, thousands after thousands of sightseers crowded into the Tuileries to examine the havoc in the royal apartments. They gloated over the bloodstained wreckage of the beautiful furniture and pointed out to each other the bullet holes that scarred the walls. The Swiss guards and the nobles still lay where they had fallen.

Nor were these sightseers all sanculottes. Many were neatly dressed, polite, and well mannered; citizens who belonged to the respectable middle class. Yet all were united by their common hatred of the King. All of them rejoiced because he and the hated Marie Antoinette had finally been driven from their palace and were now held, like common prisoners, at the mercy of the people.

Still, destroying a system of government is comparatively easy. Creating a new one is more difficult. By manipulating the hatred of the mob, the Jacobins had succeeded in destroying the monarchy. They had also destroyed the constitution which the previous Assembly had taken two years to draw up.

How then was France to be governed? Who was to rule now? These questions had to be answered and so a new cry arose. There must be yet another election to elect new deputies who would draw up a new constitution, this time without a king.

This election was actually never held. The men who were soon to seize power could not risk having it taken from them by the voters. Besides, holding an election takes time, and France needed a new government immediately, for the ministers appointed by the King had to be replaced. On August 10, the day after the attack on the Tuileries, the Assembly appointed a temporary executive council to govern France.

This council consisted of six men. Five of them, including Roland, were either Girondins or other moderate revolutionaries. Although the Commune, which governed the city of Paris, had been taken over by the Jacobins, the moderate deputies still made up a majority of the Assembly. However, the sixth member of the council was a Jacobin. He was Georges Danton, and he was to become one of the most important and perhaps the greatest of all the leaders who came and went during the Revolution.

Danton was a curious mixture. He came from a respectable country family and had been a prosperous lawyer before the Revolution began. Nonetheless, he hated the aristocrats and despised the respectable bourgeois. His sympathies were with the poor working men and women of the cities. Generous-minded and honestly distressed by the sufferings of the poor, he wanted everyone to share in the benefits of the Revolution.

Danton's most impressive characteristic was his enormous vitality. He was a tall man who towered over his companions, with a massive chest and huge shoulders, and a booming voice so powerful that it could carry across several streets. His face, pockmarked with smallpox, was exceedingly ugly. Yet he possessed great charm. He was a good scholar and enjoyed reading. Unlike the scholarly Girondins, however, whose ideas came largely from books, Danton understood instinctively the thoughts and feelings of ordinary men and women. That was one reason why he was so popular. People also liked his gaiety, his exuberant vitality, his friendliness, his generosity. At the same time, they feared him, for they knew how ruthlessly he would sweep aside anyone who stood in his way. He was perfectly capable of sending hundreds of innocent people to their death if he believed it would help the Revolution. And unfortunately he was not an honest man. Although he sympathized with the poor and hated the rich bourgeois, he himself liked to live in luxury, in a big house, with plenty of good food to eat and wine to drink. "The Revolution is a battle," he once said. "Shall it not be followed, like all battles, by a division of the spoils among the conquerors?" As one of the "conquerors," Danton is said to have taken huge bribes to pay for the luxuries he so much enjoyed. And yet, though he could be ruthless and cruel and dishonest, he was also a very tender-hearted man. Of all his pleasures, he was probably happiest sitting quietly with the wife he loved in the peaceful beauty of their country garden.

This curious mixture of a man was soon to prove himself the savior of the Revolution. At that moment, France needed a man of such demonic energy to save Paris from the enemy armies. The Austrians stood at the Belgian frontier while, farther to the east, the armies of Prussia had advanced to within a hundred miles of Paris.

The Prussians were commanded by the Duke of Brunswick, a stupid, arrogant bully of a man who hated the Revolution and all its talk of liberty and equality. Some weeks before the second attack on the Tuileries Palace, Brunswick had issued an official threat that if either Louis or any of his family were harmed, his soldiers would execute everyone responsible. No one in Paris doubted that he would carry out his threat if his men reached Paris, and his approach aroused terror among the Parisians. In this mood the revolutionaries in the city were more ready than ever to listen to the warnings of the Jacobins. The city, the Jacobins kept saying, was still filled with enemies of the Revolution — aristocrats and priests who would help Brunswick capture Paris. Then they would tell the Prussians exactly who ought to be punished for his revolutionary activities.

No one ever explained exactly who these enemies of the Revolution were or what they were plotting. But no such explanations were necessary because the people of Paris were much too frightened to bother about obtaining proof of the counterrevolutionary plots. The Prussians and the émigré nobles were coming: that was certain. To meet their attack would be difficult enough. It would be completely impossible if enemies of the Revolution, still at large in Paris, were left free to stir up trouble inside the capital. Therefore they had to be executed, and at once.

That was the Jacobins' argument and there was no shortage of potential victims. At the top of the list came the Swiss guards and the nobles who had fought to defend the Tuileries and had killed revolutionary soldiers. They, clearly, were enemies of the Revolution and had to be wiped out.

For several weeks a manhunt raged through Paris as the Swiss and the aristocrats who had managed to escape from the Tuileries were hunted down, captured and thrown into jail. While the manhunt was in progress, the moderates in Paris suffered another heavy blow; news reached the capital that Lafayette had deserted the army and had ridden over to join the enemy. Actually, Lafayette had deserted because he would fight no longer to defend a Revolution that was being taken over by the toughs and cutthroats of the Paris mob. But his desertion was a great stroke of luck for the Jacobins. He had been given his command, they pointed out, while the Girondins were in power. If he were a traitor, might not his Girondin friends be traitors also?

Skillfully, the Jacobins used Lafayette's desertion as proof that anyone who opposed them must be an enemy of the Revolution. And if a man like Lafayette were a traitor, there must surely be hundreds more like him in Paris. Under pressure from the Jacobin deputies, the Assembly therefore set up a Committee of Vigilance whose job was to ferret out all the traitors in Paris.

At this point, another man who was to become one of the most powerful of the revolutionary leaders saw his chance. Jean-Paul Marat had himself elected to the Committee of Vigilance and immediately made himself its most important member. Marat was unlike Danton in almost every possible way. He was a tiny, deformed creature, almost a dwarf, who suffered from a horrible skin disease which, some people say, he had developed when hiding from the police in the sewers of Paris. He dressed in rags and seemed never to wash, so that his foul-smelling body was caked in filth. His mind was as vicious as his body was filthy. He was consumed with hatred and envy. Before the Revolution he had been a doctor and inventor. Considering himself to be a genius, he became bitter because no one seemed to appreciate him. He envied and hated the nobles because they were powerful while he was weak. He envied and hated the prosperous bourgeois because they had money while he was poor. He even hated and envied many of his fellow revolutionaries, such as Danton, because they were popular while practically everyone who knew Marat detested him.

The Revolution gave Marat a perfect opportunity to take revenge on the kind of people who had always despised him. He became a journalist and published a daily newspaper which he called *The Friend of the People.* Writing every word of it himself, he filled it with attacks against everyone who occupied a position of power — Louis and Marie Antoinette, Mirabeau and Lafayette, Brissot, Roland, and the other Girondins. Against all of them Marat spewed out his venom. "I am the rage of the people," he declared, and no insult was too vile for him to use.

Day after day, Marat proclaimed that the rulers of France were incompetent, selfish and stupid. Unfortunately, he usually turned out to be right. For years he had been declaring that the only way to give France a good government was to find and slaughter the traitors — those mysterious traitors the Jacobins were always condemning. At first few people had taken him very seriously. But by the fall of 1792, the Paris mob was ready to believe that Marat had been right all along, and they came to trust him.

In his own way, Marat did care about the very poor. He

spent almost all of what little money he possessed on his
newspaper. He worked at it with all his might. If he did ever
happen to have a few francs to spare, he did not spend them
on himself. Instead he would give the money to some starving
wretch even poorer than himself. And, busy as he was, he
somehow found the time to listen to the grievances of any
sansculottes who came to see him.

The result was exceedingly curious. Almost everyone who
knew Marat personally detested him. Even his fellow Jacobins loathed the sight of his filthy, smelly, diseased body,
and preferred not to sit near him in the Assembly. If Marat
happened to take a seat near any of the moderate deputies,
they would immediately get up and move away. Yet, to the
sansculottes of Paris, Marat was a hero. He was their trusted
friend and spokesman who hated the rich as much as they
did. They adored him and trusted him and were ready to
carry out almost any orders he might give.

Undoubtedly Marat was a fanatic. Perhaps he was a madman. But he was also fiendishly clever and he knew exactly
what he wanted: vengeance against the kind of successful,
popular and prosperous people whom he hated and whom he
honestly believed to be enemies of the common people. Under
his leadership, the Committee of Vigilance acted with breath-
taking speed. The prisons of Paris were cleared and into the
empty cells were flung the few noblemen still left in Paris,
together with the nonjuring priests. Most of the new prisoners, however, were simply ordinary citizens whom Marat's
committee had named as traitors. In other words, the members of the committee — and especially Marat — were able to
order the arrest of anybody they disliked or wanted out of
the way.

The scene was now set for the prison massacres. To this

D

day, no one knows exactly how they started. Somebody must have organized them and almost certainly that person was the ferocious dwarf-like Marat. The massacres began one Sunday afternoon early in September. Several carriages filled with priests, and escorted by members of the National Guard, were delivering their cargo of prisoners to the Abbaye prison. Just outside the prison gates, the carriages were stopped by a menacing crowd of ill-dressed Parisian toughs, holding clubs and waving swords. From the first carriage, a priest was forced to descend. For a moment no one moved. Then the priest, reading murder in the eyes of the mob, murmured, "Mercy, mercy." As if his words had broken a spell, the mob rushed forward and cut him down with a dozen strokes of their sabers.

That first murder unleashed the violence of the mob. The hoodlums were like sharks whose appetite is aroused by the scent of blood. Rushing forward, they dragged the other priests down from their carriages and butchered them in the street. As for the National Guards who were supposed to be guarding the prisoners . . . they simply stood idly by, making no effort to interfere with the slaughter.

From the Abbaye, the mob surged through the streets to a convent called the Carmes which had been converted into a prison. There, about a hundred and fifty priests had been imprisoned. Hearing the shouts and threats of murder as the crowd pushed in at the gates of the Carmes, some of the priests retired into the garden of the convent, to kneel and offer up prayers. They were murdered as they knelt. Some of the other priests tried to escape, and a game of grisly hide-and-seek was played between pursuers and pursued among the trees of the garden before the priests were finally caught and murdered.

By this time Stanislaus Maillard had appeared at the prison. He had been one of the leaders of the attack on the Bastille and he was an ardent revolutionary. Probably he was sent to the prison by the Commune in order to give an appearance of law and order to the massacres. Maillard wasted no time. He had a table placed in the corridor that led from the convent building into the garden, and there he sat in the role of self-appointed judge. The priests who had so far escaped attack were led up before him in pairs. Without listening to their appeals, Maillard curtly ordered them "condemned" as traitors to the Revolution. As soon as he had given his verdict, the priests were pushed down a set of steps into the garden where the sansculottes were waiting to kill them.

It was almost nightfall when the massacres at the Carmes ended. Maillard and his men returned to the Abbaye prison where butchery had begun that afternoon. Inside the Abbaye there were about three hundred prisoners, most of them priests. All had been arrested in the past few days by order of Marat's committee. And all were waiting in terror, for rumors of the massacres had already spread throughout the prison.

Inside the courtyard of the Abbaye, two huge bonfires were lit to illuminate the table where Maillard sat to hold his court. Behind and around him, stood a circle of sansculottes holding their torches aloft. One after the other, the priests were led in front of Maillard and to each one of them he put one single question: "Did you take the oath?"

Everyone knew that the answer must be "no," for only those priests who had refused to take the oath had been seized and imprisoned. After receiving his answer, Maillard replied: "Let him be released." Believing himself to be free and hardly able to believe his good fortune, the prisoner followed his guards into the prison courtyard, and there he saw the other priests who had been "released." Some were already dead, their arms or legs hacked clean from their bodies. Others, not yet dead, filled the garden with their groans of agony. Hardly had the new arrival had time to realize that the same fate awaited him, when he was pushed down into the courtyard and slaughtered. Often one man would knock the condemned man unconscious; a second would cut off his head; then a third would skewer the head to the end of his pike and hold it aloft for all to see.

All night the slaughter continued until the blood of the victims flowed out of the prison courtyard and into the street which ran alongside. Meanwhile, the great majority of Parisians remained completely unaware that the massacres were taking place. One such citizen, happening to pass by the Abbaye prison on his way home from the theater, was surprised to hear the sound of shouts and screams, and to see lights flickering above the prison courtyard. Approaching a group of women who were standing on a street corner, he asked if they could explain the noise.

"Do you mean," said one of the women, "that you don't know they're taking care of the goods in the prisons?" And she pointed to the gutter near where they were standing. Following her gaze, the young man looked down and saw that a thick stream of red, sticky liquid was running along the gutter, like rain after a shower.

"It ran red," he wrote later, "with the blood of the poor creatures whom they were butchering in the Abbaye. Their cries were mingled with the yells of the executioners, and the light which I had caught a glimpse of was the light of bonfires which the murderers had lit to illuminate their exploits."

Next day the massacres spread to the other prisons of Paris. In some, a judge, either self-appointed or sent by the Commune, would sit and pronounce the sentence of death. In others, the mob simply stormed into the prisons, broke into the cells, and slaughtered the occupants. They murdered the priests. They murdered the Swiss guards and the nobles who had been caught after escaping from the Tuileries Palace and had not yet been executed. They murdered the people whom Marat and his friends disliked and had arranged to have arrested. In fact, they slaughtered everyone they could find, including ordinary petty criminals, such as pickpockets and housebreakers, who had been condemned to prison and, to their misfortune, had not been released.

The massacres were carried out by only a few hundred executioners. Many of them were paid for their work by Marat and his friends: paid in notes which were often soaked by the blood of their victims. Who were these murderous, savage executioners? Some were criminals who had been freed from the jails to make room for the men and women condemned by Marat's committee. These jailbirds were quite ready to help in the massacres in return for a few francs. So were many of the sansculottes, the hoodlums from the Paris slums who hated anyone better off than themselves. Yet a large number of the executioners were respectable, hard-working citizens. There were jewelers and wheelwrights among them, shoemakers and butchers. They joined in the massacres because they, too, hated the bourgeois and the priests; and because they were caught up, like savages, in the lust for blood that had broken out over Paris.

As the horrible work continued, members of the Committee of Vigilance traveled around the prisons, praising the executioners and urging them on: "Brave citizens," shouted one such deputy, visiting the Abbaye prison. "You are wiping out the enemies of liberty. You are doing your duty. Go on with your work."

Always the excuse was the same: the prisoners were traitors. They were friends of the émigré nobles, engaged in plots to overthrow the Revolution. If the Revolution was to be saved, the traitors must be put to death. In their hatred, the executioners exulted triumphantly over the men and women who had once been their masters and mistresses and were now their helpless victims.

One such victim was an aristocrat who had been minister of foreign affairs under Louis the Sixteenth. When he heard that he was to be moved to another prison, the aristocrat asked for his carriage.

"It is waiting, monsieur," replied one of the sansculottes with a mocking bow. A moment later and the aristocrat had been taken outside and slashed to pieces.

The most horrible murder of all was still to come. In the prison of La Force there was one prisoner whose name was known to everyone in Paris. The Princesse de Lamballe was the closest friend of the hated Marie Antoinette. She, like many other noblewomen, had fled from France but later she had chosen to return to be with her beloved Queen. With the other aristocrats she had been seized, and on Monday, the second day of the massacres, she was brought out of her prison cell to be judged.

The judge, Jacques-René Hébert, was, like Marat, a journalist. But his paper was even more violent than Marat's *Friend of the People*. It was made up almost entirely of the most vicious imaginable insults against everyone Hébert hated. Day after day, Hébert wrote vile stories, all quite untrue, about the royal family and especially about Marie Antoinette. It is impossible to say why Hébert was so full of venom. Obviously he was a kind of madman who could satisfy himself only by stirring up hatred and, unfortunately, in times of revolution there are almost always some people of his type who achieve positions of power.

It was in front of this man that the Princesse de Lamballe appeared on that Monday afternoon. Gentle and shy, she had once been among the most beautiful and charming women in France. Now her face was pale and marked with lines of heavy strain.

Hébert came brutally to the point. "Who are you?"

"Marie Thérèse Louise de Savoie-Carignan. Princesse de Lamballe."

"What is your position?"

"Superintendent of the Queen's household."

Hébert sneered at the mention of the Queen. "Swear to love liberty and equality," he ordered, "and hate the King and Queen, and royalty."

"I would willingly swear the first oath," the Princess replied. "But I cannot swear the other. It is not in my heart."

"Let her be dismissed."

The Princess, thinking she was to be freed, gave a gasp of unbelieving relief. Two guides led her to a heavy door, leading to the street, and flung it open. Stepping through the doorway, she saw that she was facing a line of corpses. The Princess could not restrain a cry of horror. But, gripping her arms, the guards forced her to walk over the corpses until, halfway across the grisly pile, she fainted. While she lay unconscious, her clothes were stripped from her body.

When she came to, the Princess found herself naked. A crowd of sansculottes surrounded her, many of them drunk, and all screaming with brutal laughter. Then one of them stepped forward and swung a club down on her head. Immediately the others rushed on her also, stabbing at her with pikes as if all were eager to share in the pleasure of driving a weapon into her body. Her head was cut off and several members of the mob carried it with them to a tavern where they forced the tavern keeper to drink a toast to the dead princess's health. Somebody then suggested that the head should be shown to its owner's dear friend, the Queen. Joyfully the idea was taken up. The princess's head was stuck on the end of a pike and carried in the middle of a jubilant crowd toward the Temple, where Marie Antoinette was kept prisoner.

On the way, another sansculotte had a further idea. He suggested that the princess's head should first be taken to a hairdresser to be curled and powdered. Under threats from the mob, the hairdresser carefully curled and powdered the blonde hair, caked as it was with blood. Then the crowd set out to the Temple where the princess's head was raised on the end of a pike and waved in front of the window of the Queen's chamber.

According to one report, Marie Antoinette, hearing the noise outside, actually went to the window and found herself staring at the head of her closest friend. Another report says that friends who were at her side tried to keep the Queen from going to the window. Filled with anguish, Marie Antoinette asked what was being kept from her, and was answered by a hostile official who was also in the room: "They want to hide from you the head of the Lamballe which has been brought here to show you how the people takes its revenge on tyrants."

But before she heard the end of his speech, Marie Antoinette fainted.

This hideous story of the Princesse de Lamballe shows the depth of the hate and viciousness produced by the Revolution in Paris. For six days and nights the massacres continued. No one knows exactly how many people were murdered. Some reports say fifteen hundred; others, as many as four thousand. But Marat was still not satisfied. He was determined that all the people he regarded as enemies of the Revolution should suffer the same fate all over France. He therefore sent out a memorandum to every town in the country urging the revolutionaries everywhere to follow the example set by the capital.

"We will march against the enemy," he declared, by which he meant the Austrians and the Prussians. "But we will not leave these criminals behind to murder our wives and children."

This, of course, was nonsense. No one slaughtered in the massacres had had any intention of murdering anybody's wife or children. Marat's memorandum was simply a further attempt to stir up hatred and to gain revenge against the kind of prosperous citizens whom he himself hated so bitterly. Thus did one of the most important of the new leaders of France urge on his fellow countrymen to murder. And still the real terror had hardly yet begun.

Although Georges Danton was not responsible for the massacres, he must certainly have known about them. Marat hated the Girondins so viciously that he wanted to arrest and execute them also, but Danton managed to prevent him. Otherwise, Danton kept himself aloof from the massacres and devoted all his enormous energies to saving France from the foreign invaders.

D*

Even while the massacres were at their peak, Danton had been working feverishly to organize the defenses of Paris. The Austrians had paused at the Belgian frontier. Further to the east, the Prussian army had also paused. It waited until the harvest was ripe so that the soldiers could collect food from the fields as they advanced. In August, the Prussians began to move forward again.

It seemed that nothing could stop Brunswick and his men from entering Paris and carrying out the Duke's threat to destroy the capital and murder the revolutionaries. The Girondins, always rather uncertain, were rapidly losing their nerve. The pompous Roland in particular was falling to pieces. He had come to suspect that his wife, whom he loved, had fallen in love with another man, as indeed she had; and his gnawing suspicion helped shatter his nerve. Rising in the Assembly, he suggested that the government should flee from Paris, taking the King with them as a hostage.

Then Danton rose. His voice, thundering across the chamber, was rich with scorn. "I want you to know," he said, speaking directly to Roland, "that I have sent for my mother, who is seventy years old, to have her brought to Paris. I have sent for my two small children; they arrived yesterday. Before the Prussians enter Paris, I want my family to perish with me. I want to see twenty thousand torches make Paris a heap of ashes. Roland, be careful how you talk of escape, make sure the people do not hear you."

With his confidence and vitality, Danton restored the shaken nerves of the Assembly and of the people. Day and night he worked with such ferocious energy and complete assurance that he became undisputed master of the government. Officials, who despised the Girondins for their inefficiency, rushed to obey Danton's orders. He appealed to the people of Paris to march out of the city and dig trenches to halt the Prussian advance. The Parisians obeyed. He arranged for every available factory to be put to work, turning out the desperately needed guns and ammunition. He called for more volunteers for the army and, from all parts of France, volunteers came, were organized rapidly into regiments and marched off to the front to hold off the invaders.

Speaking in the Assembly, Danton gave the Revolution its most inspiring motto. It was the very day on which the prison massacres had begun, and the guns of the enemy could be heard in Paris as they fired on the city of Verdun only forty miles from the capital. All gates leading out of Paris were closed. The church bells were set ringing. On the steps of public buildings, couriers read out proclamations urging all good patriots to collect muskets and march to the front. Though many of the people were shaking with fear, Danton refused even to consider the possibility of defeat.

"The tocsin you hear today," he shouted, "is not an alarm but an alert. It sounds the charge against the enemies of our country. For victory, we must dare and dare and dare again. So France will be saved."

Dare and dare and dare again. That was the spirit of Danton. To sustain the people's hopes, he promised that Verdun, the last barrier on the way to Paris, would not be given up. But, even as he spoke, he had received the news that Verdun had already fallen. Now the road to Paris lay open to the Prussian invaders.

The French army which faced the Prussians was divided into two groups. One was commanded by General Kellermann, the other by General Dumouriez who had been given his command because he was a personal friend of the Girondins. Both generals knew that their men were too raw and undisciplined to launch an attack against the well-trained Prussians. They therefore decided to wait, and they lined up their troops along the top of a hill on either side of a windmill at the village of Valmy.

Brunswick could have marched his army past the French and on into Paris. But he was afraid to leave an undefeated army, however weak, behind his lines. Besides, he thought it impossible that a ragged collection of Frenchmen, short of officers and racked by lack of discipline, could stand up against his own soldiers. A single charge up the hill would make them flee as they had fled from the Austrians in Belgium. So it seemed to Brunswick, and he decided to attack.

For days rain had fallen in a heavy downpour on the countryside around Valmy. But on the day before Brunswick's attack, it had stopped falling. When dawn broke, a heavy mist lay across the hill where the French were standing and over the valley which separated them from the Prussians.

Gradually, the mist cleared and Brunswick was able to see the French, in their positions along the hilltop. Unlike the soldiers of a well-trained army, they were not drawn up in one long even line. Instead they were gathered in scattered groups. Some of the soldiers had no caps. Others were without boots. A few were properly uniformed but many wore trousers of one uniform and tunics of another. And many were still dressed in the civilian jerseys and trousers which they had worn as they marched away from Paris.

At the sight of this ragged and tattered army, Brunswick's confidence increased. He ordered his cannon to open fire. At that range, most of the cannonballs fell wide. Even so some of the French scattered and fled.

Then Brunswick gave the order to advance. In neat, long lines, with their muskets and the buttons on their uniforms glittering in the sun, the Prussian grenadiers moved down from their hill and into the valley toward the French. Steadily they moved forward, to within eight hundred, six hundred, five hundred yards of the French . . .

At last Dumouriez ordered his few pieces of artillery to fire. Cannonballs ripped into the Prussian lines. Dumouriez ordered his infantrymen to join in; there was a crackle of muskets and a few more Prussians fell. Still the casualties were light. The main body of the enemy remained unharmed. Onward and onward the Prussians advanced. If they could reach the top of the hill, not one of them doubted that they would put the French to rout.

But the Prussians never did reach the top of the hill. Gradually, their advance slackened, the men moving more and more slowly until they came almost to a halt. The crash of the French cannon and the rattle of French muskets grew more fierce. Now considerable numbers of Prussians were falling. Halfway up the hill their line halted. The men could go no further. Angry and bewildered, Brunswick gave the order to retreat.

Why had the attack failed? What Brunswick failed to realize was that the land in the valley was ploughland from which the harvest had recently been cleared. The heavy rain of the past few days had turned the soil to mud. With every step, the Prussian grenadiers had found it more and more difficult to drag their feet through the mud until finally movement became such an effort that their will to advance disappeared.

Still, the Prussian army remained very much stronger than the French, and Dumouriez was sure that Brunswick would attack again the next day. He was wrong. On the slopes leading up to Valmy, the Prussian advance had reached its furthest limit. Instead of launching another attack, the next day Brunswick ordered his men to retreat from Paris.

Actually, the Prussian army was not as formidable as the French had thought. The men were tired. They had marched too far from their bases. They were short of food and supplies and a serious outbreak of disease was spreading death among them. Moreover the Prussians were not truly anxious to capture Paris. If they could have overcome the French without having to fight a real battle, they would have done so. But the prospect of a hard fight and the risk of more deaths from disease changed their minds.

"Why should we die," they asked themselves, "to put a foreign king back on his throne? Why should we die so that these arrogant French nobles should be able to win back their estates?"

The French émigrés who had accompanied Brunswick's army were livid with disappointment and fury. But their fury was in vain. Brunswick refused to listen to their appeals to continue his advance toward Paris, and insisted on carrying through his retreat to the frontier.

In Paris the news of the victory at Valmy came as a sensation. At first the people of the capital could hardly believe that they were really safe. Ten days after the battle, the American Ambassador to France, Gouverneur Morris, still could not understand that the powerful Prussian army had been driven back by the ragged legions of the Revolution. But, as events were soon to show, the battle of Valmy, in which only a few hundred men had died, was the decisive battle of the Revolution and, indeed, one of the most important battles in history.

The German poet Goethe was at Valmy, and he for one did

understand the tremendous importance of what had happened when the Prussian advance slowed and halted. Paris, he realized, was safe from conquest and the Revolution could not now be overturned.

"Here and today," wrote Goethe, "began a new age in the history of the world." He was right. With their successful revolution against the King and his aristocratic friends, the French had proved that a people could control its own destiny. It was a lesson that the other people of Europe would soon learn, and that they would not forget.

Engraved by W H Mote

ROBESPIERRE

# CHAPTER SEVEN

# THE KING IS EXECUTED

T HE BATTLE of Valmy had saved Paris and freed its people from the dread fear that the émigré nobles would return in triumph and carry out a terrible revenge on the revolutionaries. Yet the French victory did not improve the situation in Paris. It had the opposite effect. It made things worse.

Similar situations occur frequently in history. When a country is in mortal danger from some outside enemy, its people tend to unite in their common fear. They forget their differences, and work together to defeat the enemy. But when the danger disappears, so does the fear. Then politicians and their supporters go back to squabbling and fighting against each other.

This is what happened in Paris in the fall of 1792. With the Prussians only forty miles from Paris, the Parisians had been so scared that they forgot their differences. It is true that Marat and his bloodthirsty assistants had seized on the atmosphere of fear to massacre many of the people they hated. But only a few hundred Parisians had taken part in the massacres. The others had concentrated on the great task of saving their capital from the invading Prussians.

But as soon as it became clear that Paris was safe, the struggle between the Girondins and the Jacobins broke out again with renewed fury. There was good reason for it. With every month that passed, the government of France was drifting into a state of more hopeless chaos.

In fact there was no real government left at all. In September, the Assembly declared that Louis was no longer king and that the monarchy had been abolished. This meant that the revolutionary constitution was shattered, just as the United States Constitution would be if, say, the Congress decided that we were no longer to have a President. Somehow the French had to create a new form of government. So the Assembly decided that another election should be held to elect deputies to a National Convention which would then draw up a new constitution.

The Convention was elected and its members thereupon became the new masters of France. Since the King had been deposed, the Convention was the only legal instrument of government in the country. There were, of course, local governments in the towns and villages. But only the Convention exercised power over the country as a whole.

Actually, the Convention never did get around to setting up a new legal form of government. Its members were too busy running the country and settling their own quarrels. From the start, a vicious struggle for power broke out between the Girondins on the one hand, and the Jacobins on the other. Numerically, the Girondins were the stronger because the majority of Frenchmen lived in small towns or in the countryside, and they tended to support the Girondins. As the Convention had been elected by the whole nation, the Girondin deputies and their allies greatly outnumbered the Jacobin deputies. The administration continued to be controlled by the executive council which was made up of a group of Girondins, together with Georges Danton.

Danton, being a Jacobin, was an extreme revolutionary; however, he was a minister and most of his energy went into trying to keep the government going and, especially, making the army strong. The other Jacobins formed what we would call the opposition. They had no responsibilities and their principal aim was to destroy the Girondins and seize power for themselves.

At this point, another Jacobin leader, Maximilien Robespierre, gradually began to emerge as one of the most powerful men in France. He is very difficult to describe and, ever since the Revolution, historians have argued endlessly about him. On the surface, he didn't seem to possess the qualities of either a leader or an extreme revolutionary. He was a lawyer, a typical member of the bourgeois, and he looked it. His manner was like Roland's: prim and stiff and prissy. He was not loud and boisterous, like Danton, or filthy and uncouth, like Marat. Instead he was quiet and reserved and the last word in respectability. He dressed always in plain, dark clothes, and he even wore the traditional silk breeches — the culottes — which the poor people of Paris so despised.

Yet they trusted him as much as they trusted their idol, Marat. One reason was that Robespierre lived very simply in a small house, as a lodger with a respectable middle-class family. No one could ever accuse him of taking bribes, as Danton was supposed to do. So great was Robespierre's reputation for honesty that he became known as Robespierre the Incorruptible. Moreover, Robespierre was very clever at getting many different groups to support him. He attacked the Girondins as viciously as Marat did, and that made him popular with the hoodlums of the Paris slums. At the same time, he was continually making speeches about how people should work hard, and save their money, and live simple, virtuous lives. And that made him popular with the Parisians who were not very well off, but who did work hard, and who thought that being respectable was tremendously important.

Robespierre also possessed a quality which is extremely rare and which had a great deal to do with making him so powerful. He was able to terrify his enemies. How he did this, no one has ever been able to explain. He was not an inspiring speaker. He spoke in a low, monotonous voice and his speeches were almost always long-winded and dull. Yet somehow he managed to convey the impression that anyone who opposed him was taking a terrible risk. Perhaps his opponents sensed that, underneath his quiet, prim exterior, Robespierre was totally ruthless and would destroy anyone, even his closest friend, who stood in his way. Although he probably did not realize it himself, Robespierre was obsessed with a lust for power. Unlike Danton, he had no pleasures. He enjoyed nothing. Politics was his only interest and he possessed a fantastic amount of determination and willpower. In times of revolution and chaos, ruling a country efficiently becomes so difficult that only men with an almost insane lust for power can manage to do it. That is one reason why so many extraordinary people rose to the top during the French Revolution. But none were stranger than Marat, the diseased, hate-filled dwarf, and that grim, merciless figure, Robespierre the Incorruptible, who burned inside with an unquenchable lust for power and possessed that mysterious gift, as he looked up suddenly over his glasses, of provoking fear in almost everyone who caught his gaze.

For several weeks after the dethronement of Louis, the Convention was filled with accusations and threats as these men and their followers battled the Girondins. For the moment, Danton was safe. He was a national hero and no one dared to criticize him. But slowly, inevitably, the Girondins, now led by Roland, and the Jacobins, led by Marat and Robespierre, were drawn on into an ever more desperate struggle which could be ended only by the destruction of one side or the other.

The Jacobins' main strength lay in their control over the Paris mob. Recognizing that the Girondins were supported by a great majority of the French people, the Jacobins were not yet ready to lead the mob in an open uprising against them. But the threat was always there, and the Girondins knew it. If hoodlums from the Paris slums could overthrow the monarchy, they might also be able to overthrow the legally elected Convention. Somehow, the Girondins decided, they had to win the confidence of the poor people of Paris.

The method they adopted was Roland's idea and he thought it a very clever one. The Jacobins were insisting that Louis the Tyrant, as they called him, should be brought to trial for treason — for trying to destroy the Revolution. To prove that he and his fellow Girondins were truly sincere and ardent revolutionaries, Roland decided to launch the attack on Louis himself.

Like the summoning of the men from Marseilles to Paris, this decision turned out to be a terrible mistake. By bringing Louis to trial, the Girondins played right into the hands of Robespierre and Marat. But Roland, who was mainly responsible, was really a very stupid man and he simply failed to foresee what would happen.

Actually there was plenty of evidence to show that Louis had tried to overthrow the Revolution. Everyone knew that when he attempted to escape from France, he had planned to return at the head of an Austrian army. There was also a great deal of other evidence against Louis, most of it in the form of documents which were found hidden inside a secret safe in his room in the Tuileries Palace. Some of the documents were letters Louis had exchanged with nonjuring priests. Others consisted of copies of letters which he and his ministers had written to the Austrians, while planning an invasion of France. Others showed that Louis had tried to bribe the city officials of Paris to stop the attack that had been launched against the Tuileries Palace.

Bribes! Secret invasion plans! Plots with the hated priests! The evidence which Roland presented to the Convention was damning. The documents found in Louis's safe proved that right from the beginning Louis had been scheming to destroy the revolutionaries. Without any argument, the members of the Convention decided that Louis should be brought before them to be tried for treason.

The trial was short. Louis, now known simply as Louis Capet (the old family name of the French kings), was brought to the floor of the Convention chamber. Plainly dressed in a coat of olive-colored silk, he sat in a wooden armchair and calmly answered all the charges that were hurled at him. The accusations, he said, were false. He had never tried to betray the Revolution. The documents said to have been found in his secret safe were forgeries. Only once did he display any strong emotion. A deputy shouted that he had been responsible for shedding the blood of Frenchmen, and Louis replied in a voice that shook with indignation: "No, sir. I have never shed the blood of Frenchmen."

That was true. If Louis had been ready to order the shedding of a little blood, he would probably have still been King. But no one in the Convention believed any of his other denials, and indeed Louis must have been lying. He had — and everybody knew it — plotted to regain his former power, and, to the members of the Convention, that made him guilty of treason.

But that decision raised an extremely difficult question. What was to be done with him? How was he to be punished? After all, Louis had once been the King of France, a man revered almost as if he were a god. Could such a man be executed because he had tried to save his throne?

It was at this moment that the Girondins realized with horror that they had led themselves into a terrible trap. Marat, Robespierre, Danton and the other Jacobins knew exactly what they wanted done; they wanted Louis to be executed. So did the Paris mob, the very people whom the Girondins had hoped to conciliate by bringing the King to trial. If they were to please the mob, they would have to vote for Louis's death. But they were men of moderation who hated the idea of execution. Moreover, they had tried to work with Louis; they had served as his ministers even after he had been brought back in disgrace from Varennes.

Everyone, inside the Convention and outside, knew that the Girondins hated the idea of voting to put Louis to death. There lay their dilemma. If they voted against executing Louis, they would earn yet more hatred from the Paris mob. But if they voted for his execution, they would be doing so, not from conviction but from fear. They would show themselves to be weaklings without the courage to stand up for their beliefs. They would lose the support of the moderate men of France who felt as they did. And they would also, by revealing such weakness, encourage their enemies to increase their attacks.

Late on the evening of January 17, 1793, in an atmosphere

of tremendous tension and excitement, the voting began. Three great chandeliers cast a dim light over the long, narrow chamber and the deputies crammed close together on their wooden benches. At one end was the rostrum which every deputy had to mount to deliver his verdict and, if he wished, give reasons for it. Every place was taken in the balcony which ran around the walls of the chamber. Some of the spectators were sansculottes and their women, raggedly dressed, and as animated and happy as if they were watching an exciting game. Refreshing themselves from bottles of wine, they eagerly scanned the faces of the deputies, cheering or booing as each one delivered his verdict, and keeping careful record of the score. The section of balcony at the far end of the chamber, opposite the rostrum, was filled with citizens of a better class, and they were more relaxed. They behaved as if they were sitting in boxes at a theater. Watching them, no one could possibly have guessed that below them, a former king was on trial for his life. They sucked on oranges and ices. They drank liqueurs. Chatting gaily, they moved around the balcony, visiting and greeting their friends. And all around the balcony, and in the coffee houses which surrounded the Convention chamber, men exchanged bets on what the result of the voting would be.

One by one, the deputies mounted the rostrum.

"Death," said one.

"Banishment," declared another.

"Imprisonment for life," announced a third.

For almost twenty-four hours, the voting continued while spectators came and went in the galleries. On the floor of the chamber, thick and foul with stale air, deputies dozed off and had to be awakened when their turn came to vote. Yet despite the growing weariness, everyone came sharply to life when Robespierre walked to the rostrum.

"I hate the penalty of death," he said virtuously, in his low, monotonous tones. "But I know nothing of that humanity which is forever sacrificing whole peoples and protecting tyrants. I vote for death."

Marat came to the rostrum. "Death," he screamed.

Then the voice of Danton was heard. Only a few days before, he had returned exhausted from inspecting the armies at the front to find that his wife, whom he loved, was dying. All that day he had sat, brokenhearted, at her bedside. His huge, powerful body sagged with fatigue and grief. Yet from the rostrum his voice, powerful as ever, rang through the chamber. "I am no politician," he shouted. "I vote for death."

And the Girondins? Faced with their agonizing dilemma, their nerve failed. Although they believed that to execute Louis was a foul and inexcusable crime, almost all their leaders voted for his execution. They were afraid that, if they expressed their true feelings, they would themselves be damned as traitors. Yet their surrender to fear was useless. The people of Paris were not deceived. They understood what was in the Girondins' hearts and despised them.

The President of the Convention on the day of the voting was Vergniaud, one of the earliest and most influential of the Girondins. He, too, had voted for Louis's execution. Yet to the end he must have hoped that Louis's life would be spared, for it was in a voice deep with gloom that he announced to the hushed chamber:

"It is with profound sadness that I declare the penalty incurred by Louis Capet to be, by the vote of a majority of the Assembly, that of death."

Some two years before, a mild-mannered doctor, Joseph Guillotin, had come up with an idea for what he called a decapitating machine. Until that time, any ordinary Frenchman condemned to death had been executed by hanging. Only members of the nobility were an exception: they were granted the special privilege of having their heads chopped off by an axe. But both these methods of execution were clumsy. Hanging took a long time; and, frequently, when a noble was executed, the man who chopped off his head had to swing his axe half a dozen times before the job was done. Dr. Guillotin's instrument was a great improvement. It worked very quickly and with great efficiency. The condemned man — or woman — lay on a slab of wood with his head clamped into position inside a wooden vice balanced over a basket. From above, a razor-sharp blade dropped like a flash between two wooden supports and crisply cut off the victim's head, which then dropped neatly into the basket.

This new instrument, named the guillotine after its inventor, was ideal for the Revolution. One revolutionary praised it because "now no man need stain his hands with the murder of his brethren." Besides, it permitted a new kind of equality: nobles and ordinary people alike could be executed in the same way, and quickly.

In Paris the guillotine was set up in the center of a huge square named the Place de la Revolution. It stood on a high platform so that the spare, wooden frame, a grim symbol of death, was starkly outlined against the sky. Here on the morning of January 21, 1793, Louis was brought to pay for his crimes against the Revolution.

Perhaps Louis had expected the verdict of death, for he took the news with that curious calmness he invariably displayed in moments of danger. He has come down through the pages of history as a strangely contradictory figure. At every crisis since the Revolution had begun, he had shown himself to be slow-witted, weak, and indecisive. Several times over, if he had possessed a fraction of his wife's firmness, he could probably have brought the Revolution to an end. Yet in moments of physical danger, he was always as cool as the most heroic of soldiers.

On the evening before he was to die, Marie Antoinette and their two children were allowed into Louis's room. For a few minutes, the former King and his wife talked together and Louis, who hated the idea of vengeance, made his young son swear never to try and avenge his father's death. That night, Louis and Marie Antoinette did not bid each other a final farewell; the former King promised faithfully that he would visit her next morning to say his last goodbye. But that meeting never took place. For Louis had loved his wife dearly, and he could not bring himself to face her tears.

At five o'clock, he awoke after a brief sleep. His priest held a final mass and Louis listened to it on his knees. Then the waiting began. With agonizing slowness, the minutes dragged by until, at about eight o'clock, the clatter of horses' hooves sounded outside the prison and General Santerre, the former brewer and now commander of the Paris National Guard, entered Louis's chamber.

"Have you come for me?" Louis asked.

"Yes," answered Santerre curtly.

Surrounded by soldiers, Louis crossed the garden outside the prison and took his place in the coach that awaited him while, from a window on the third floor, Marie Antoinette peered down on him in anguish. The procession formed. At the front, Santerre pranced proudly on the finest horse he had been able to find. Behind him came the coach, sur-

rounded on all sides by ranks of soldiers, holding their muskets at the ready. Then came the drummers, rank upon rank
of them, beating, as they marched, an endless, funereal roll.

So, slowly the procession passed through the streets, half-
concealed under a thick fog. On each side, four rows of soldiers were drawn up, standing shoulder to shoulder and on
the watch to repel any last-minute attempt that might be
made to rescue the doomed King.

Despite the elaborate precautions taken to prevent it, such
an attempt was made. One of the King's oldest friends, the
Baron de Batz, had organized a group of royalists who were
still at large in Paris, to launch a sudden attack on the procession. Their plan was to seize Louis, and carry him to
safety. As the carriage rolled past, de Batz, under the impression that his friends were ready, raised his hat above his
head as the signal for attack, and cried out:

"To us, my friends. All those who wish to save the King."

The monotonous beat of the drums drowned out de Batz's
cry. Only three or four voices replied. In an instant, a group
of soldiers had turned on the would-be rescuers. Desperately
they fled for safety down a side street, but two of them were
caught and killed while de Batz himself barely managed to
escape.

Louis, bent over his prayer book, did not even notice the
incident. As if unaware of the marching column and the silent ranks of paraded soldiers, he continued to read until the
procession passed into the Place de la Revolution. There,
twenty thousand troops stood massed in silent, serried ranks
around the guillotine, while the drums continued to beat
their persistent dreadful roll of death.

"We are there, unless I am mistaken," said Louis to the
priest who sat beside him in the carriage. The priest bowed

silently, and Louis walked through a door into the space below the platform on which the guillotine stood. He took off
his vest, opened his shirt collar, and then knelt at the priest's
feet to receive his last blessing. The executioner, Sanson,
bound his hands behind his back with a handkerchief, slashed
off his hair with a pair of scissors, and pointed to the ladder
up to the scaffold.

Slowly Louis mounted the ladder. Looking around him, he
could see the dense mass of soldiers. Suddenly, he advanced
to the edge of the platform and made a sign to the drummers
in front of him to stop their beating. In the abrupt silence
that followed, his voice rang out clearly over the square:

"Frenchmen, I die innocent. I pardon the authors of my
death, I pray God that the blood which is about to be spilt
will never fall on the head of France. And you, unhappy people . . ."

Before he could finish, an officer ordered the drummers to
recommence their beat, to drown out the King's words. Still
Louis continued to cry out to them to be silent, ceasing only
when Sanson and his assistants dragged him down and
bound him to the wooden slab. The knife flashed down the
wooden frame of the guillotine, and the head of the dead
man, formerly Louis the Sixteenth of France, dropped into
the waiting basket.

Now pandemonium broke loose as the crowd which hitherto had stood silent behind the ranks of soldiers gave themselves up to a frenzy of joy. Perhaps they truly, foolishly,
believed that the death of a helpless man would make their
Revolution more secure. A hatred and a savagery had been
unleashed in France which could be satisfied only by the
sight of slaughter. That alone can explain the extraordinary
scenes which followed Louis's death.

One of the young apprentice executioners scooped up Louis's head from the basket and walked around the platform, displaying it to the crowd. From all sides, men and women pushed their way through the soldiers and up to the platform to dip their fingers in the slain man's blood. This was the blood of Louis the tyrant and they daubed it on their foreheads to bring themselves good luck. One man was even seen to give a young boy money to take his handkerchief up to the platform and bring it back, wet and sticky with blood.

Meanwhile, in her room in the Temple, Marie Antoinette was waiting. She heard the sound of drums, first loud under her window, then slowly dying away in the distance. An hour passed and then she heard the voice of a revolutionary shouting under her window: "The tyrant is dead. Long live France. Long live the Republic."

Marie Antoinette listened for a moment, then turned and went back inside her room. She had no tears left to shed. Perhaps she was wondering how long it would be before her time would come to lose her head under the guillotine.

DUMOURIEZ

# CHAPTER EIGHT

# THE JACOBINS SEIZE POWER

---

T HE MURDER or execution of a king, a president, or any other political leader almost never produces the expected result. Thus it was with the execution of Louis. His death altered nothing. It solved no problems. The Girondins continued to cling to power even though the sansculottes of Paris now despised as well as hated them. Extreme revolutionaries like Marat continued to shout for the death of traitors to the Revolution. Meanwhile, the people of Paris and the other large cities of France were worse off than they had ever been.

As more and more men joined the armies and went off to the front, there were fewer people to buy goods. That meant fewer workers were needed to make or sell them, and so the number of people who were out of work kept growing. Prices continued to rise. Worst of all, so much food was needed for the army that less than ever could be spared for the civilians who stayed at home. In Paris the shortage of food became so severe that some people suggested that dogs and cats should be killed for their meat. They were told that, if this were done, the rats in the city would spread even faster. In their desperate need for food, mobs kept breaking out into riots,

E

storming into butcher shops and pastry shops and sometimes killing the owners. Every delivery of food into the city had to be made under a heavy escort of soldiers to keep the people from breaking open the wagons and looting them.

Marat had his usual solution, the remedy for every problem: more death. If food was short, it was because rich people were hoarding it, waiting for prices to rise even further. "Kill the hoarders," Marat demanded. "If a few were hanged, there would soon be an end to the frauds that have reduced five million men and women to despair and starvation. And what do the representatives of the people do? They chatter about these evils. But they do not present a single remedy."

The Girondins indeed had no remedy. They were like men in a sailing boat, drifting out to sea into a hurricane, and every move they made seemed only to carry France further out to where the hurricane raged most fiercely. Already the country was at war with Austria and Prussia. Now the execution of the King frightened the English, twenty miles away across the English Channel. For England was governed by a king and by aristocrats, and they began to fear that the example set by the French would spread across the Channel to their own shores.

The English had good reason to be afraid. While the French people at home were suffering through the bitter winter, the French army was winning victory after victory. Since the battle of Valmy, an astonishing change had come over the army. Through Danton's untiring efforts, more supplies had reached the soldiers, and under the skillful leadership of General Dumouriez, the hero of Valmy, the French pressed on after the retreating Austrians and Prussians. They conquered Belgium and moved close to Holland. Giddy with victory, the Convention decided to widen the war. In February of 1793, it declared war on England. In March, it declared war on Spain. The war of defense had turned into a war of conquest. In their battle against kings, the French had deliberately set every country in Western Europe against them.

This situation greatly disturbed both Danton and General Dumouriez, the two men who were mainly responsible for driving the foreign invaders back from French soil. They very soon began to realize that the French army was paying a terribly heavy price for its victories. In March, making another tour of the armies, Danton was horrified by what he found. Despite all his efforts, the men were now desperately short of food and guns and ammunition. Their uniforms were in tatters and their boots were so worn out by the constant marching, that they had to wear scarves around their feet. Worst of all, they were close to exhaustion.

Meanwhile, back in Paris, Marat was continuing to attack the Girondins, including their friend General Dumouriez. He accused Dumouriez of intending to betray the Revolution. At first, few people listened. Marat, they thought, was now going too far in condemning Dumouriez, the general who had driven the Prussians back at Valmy and thus became one of the great heroes of the Revolution.

But once again the perpetually suspicious Marat turned out to be right. For Dumouriez had lost the will to continue the war. Better than anyone, he knew that his men were growing more and more exhausted. The enemy soldiers, on the other hand, were growing steadily stronger as they retreated closer to their bases at home. Moreover, Dumouriez hated the Jacobins and it seemed to him that the Revolution had gotten completely out of hand. He therefore decided that it was his duty to dissolve the Convention and to set up a new and more moderate government.

Before Dumouriez was ready to strike, news of his plan leaked back to the Convention. Promptly the deputies sent out three emissaries to deprive Dumouriez of his command, place him under arrest, and bring him back to Paris. But when the emissaries reached him, Dumouriez arrested them instead and appealed to his soldiers to follow him back to Paris to overthrow the Convention. Now, however, Dumouriez discovered that he had misjudged the spirit of his men. They were volunteers and ardent supporters of the Revolution. To them, the members of the Convention and especially their hero, Danton, represented the spirit of the Revolution, for which they had fought and suffered. Instead of following Dumouriez, their commander, his men threatened to kill him. In order to escape, Dumouriez had to gallop for safety into the Austrian lines.

Dumouriez a deserter! The news staggered the people of Paris. It seemed incredible. But it was true and it appeared to prove that Marat had been right all along when he said that no one except the Jacobins could be trusted. Lafayette, the hero of 1789, had deserted to the enemy. Now Dumouriez, the adored hero of Valmy, had done the same.

Dumouriez, it must be remembered, had been given his command because he had been a friend of the Girondins. So, to Marat and Robespierre, his desertion came as a wonderful stroke of good fortune. Dumouriez, asserted Robespierre, was a friend of the Girondins. Dumouriez had proved himself a traitor. Therefore the Girondins, too, must be traitors. This kind of false and unfair argument is called "guilt by association." Actually, Robespierre's claim was totally unjustified because the Girondins had done and still were doing their best to help Danton wage the war. But the sansculottes of Paris trusted Robespierre and they believed him. They also trusted Marat who was doing everything possible to stir up their hatred against the Girondins.

"Your greatest enemies," he declared, "lurk amongst yourselves. They direct your operations, they direct your means of defense. The counterrevolution lies within the National Convention. Among the deputies, there are traitors and royalists. If you liberate them, our liberty is gone. If they are expelled promptly and for good, then the country is saved."

Thus Marat and Robespierre had now reached the point of accusing the Girondins of being traitors. Pause for a moment and ponder what this word "traitor" was supposed to mean. It was the Girondins who had started the war. Together with Danton, they were administering the government. Under their leadership, the French armies had won victory after victory. They had even voted for the death of Louis.

How then could they be called traitors either to France or to the Revolution? The answer is that the word traitor had ceased to mean a man who betrays his country. Instead it had come to be used simply as a term of abuse, to be hurled at any rival or enemy. The Girondins were enemies not of the Revolution but of the Jacobins. They were one group of men fighting for power against another group. But Marat and Robespierre knew very well what they were doing when they told the sansculottes that the Girondins were "traitors." For the mere word traitor called up in the minds of the sansculottes a picture of the aristocrats and the priests — those familiar bogey men of the revolutionaries. Although hardly any still remained in the city, Marat and Robespierre kept insisting that they were all over Paris, hidden away in the houses of counterrevolutionaries and holding secret meetings where they concocted fresh plots against all true revolutionaries. With these rumors, the Jacobins kept the Paris mob in a perpetual state of fear. And, by describing their rivals as traitors, they gradually brought the mob to the point where they were ready to make an all-out attack on the Girondins.

The Jacobins were not just talkers. They were also extremely efficient men of action. They were indeed one of the most brutally efficient set of leaders in history. As the number of their supporters grew, the leaders built up a tough and ruthless organization. Some of the men who joined it were fanatical revolutionaries who honestly believed what Marat and Robespierre told them. Some were Parisian hoodlums who cared little about politics but eagerly seized their chance to make themselves important. Yet others were cold-blooded opportunists who could see that the Jacobins were gaining strength and wanted to jump on the bandwagon. From all these men, the Jacobin leaders selected the most ruthless and efficient and sent them out as agents to the other big cities of France; to Lyons and Nantes and Marseilles. These agents were carefully trained. They were taught exactly how to stir up the mobs inside other cities just as their leaders had done in Paris.

Still, the assignment given to these agents was far from easy. Throughout the provinces of France, the people were becoming increasingly alarmed by the growing strength of the Jacobins. There were, first of all, the rich, conservative-minded businessmen and lawyers who had replaced the nobles as the most powerful men in France. They had taken over control of most of the local governments and they were afraid of the Jacobins; afraid that the Jacobins might take away their power, their property, and perhaps even their lives. Then there were the peasants who now owned their own plots of land and wanted to be left alone to work their farms in peace. And there were thousands of Frenchmen who had yet another cause of complaint. The supply of eager young volunteers for the army had dried up, so Danton had organized press gangs to go around the country, pick out healthy young men and force them to join the army. Their activities aroused great bitterness, for the young men's parents hated to see their sons dragged off to fight in a war that seemed to have nothing to do with them.

Especially in the country districts, there were still many supporters of the monarchy. They hated both the Girondins and the Jacobins for executing their King. Finally, there were the nonjuring priests, still powerful in the countryside, who looked on both the Girondins and the Jacobins as atheists, and longed to drive them all from power.

All these different groups bitterly resented what was happening in Paris, and in March, 1793, their bitterness flared out into open revolt. In La Vendée, a province in western France, the country people raised the flag of rebellion. They attacked and defeated the few government soldiers who were stationed there. They also declared that they would no longer pay taxes or allow their sons to be dragged off to fight in foreign wars.

The uprising in La Vendée was actually a revolt of country people against all the revolutionary leaders in Paris. But it was the Girondins who suffered the most. They had come to be regarded as the representatives of the country people, while the Jacobins were the spokesmen for the poor of Paris. It was therefore easy for the Jacobins to convince the sansculottes that the Girondins approved of the revolt in La Vendée. Skillfully Robespierre played on their suspicions.

"Only a madman," he declared, "could believe that the

friends of Dumouriez intend to fight the traitors of the
Vendée." With this kind of talk, Robespierre and his fellow
Jacobins stirred up the toughs and hoodlums of the Paris
slums to yet another violent outbreak. Less than a year
before, the mob had driven Louis from his throne. Now they
were ready to drive from power the moderate revolutionaries, the Girondins. The Revolution had become steadily
more radical — or extreme. The poorer and more desperate
people of France had grown more and more powerful while
the rich and better-educated citizens had grown steadily
weaker. Before 1789, France had been ruled by the King and
his aristocratic friends. They had been replaced by the prosperous bourgeois of the Estates-General who certainly did
not believe in revolution by violence. Their main desire had
been to take over the position of the King and the nobles as
the rulers of France. Then they in turn had been replaced by
men like the Girondins who genuinely wanted the government to provide equal opportunities for all the people. Now,
in the summer of 1793, the street mobs of Paris were ready to
turn against the Girondins and anyone else who was rich or
well educated or in any way better off than themselves.

The revolt against the Girondins was organized by yet another of the self-appointed committees which kept springing
up throughout the Revolution. Many of its members were
quite unknown. One was a printer, another a painter, a third
a toy-maker, a fourth a decorator. Probably, behind the
scenes, Robespierre and Marat were helping the committee to
rouse the Paris mob to action. On the night of May 30, the
familiar signs of disorder broke out, as the mob began to go
on the rampage. While the church bells sounded the tocsin,
the Paris toughs swarmed through the streets, smashing win-

dows, looting stores and terrorizing peaceful citizens. Meanwhile, the self-appointed revolutionary committee announced that the city of Paris had risen in revolt against tyranny: that is, against the Girondins.

Santerre, the commander of the National Guard, happened to be away from Paris. In his place, the revolutionary committee appointed an ex-clerk named François Hanriot to command the Guard. Hanriot was tough, brutal and efficient and he wasted no time. He ordered his men to fire a salvo of cannon to demonstrate that the people of Paris were once again in revolt, and perhaps to warn those who opposed it not to interfere. Then he closed all the roads leading into and out of Paris and ordered thousands of his men to surround the Convention chamber.

Inside the chamber, Jacobin deputies were demanding that twenty-two Girondin leaders must be expelled from the Convention because they were traitors to the Revolution. However, the Girondins and their supporters still outnumbered the Jacobins inside the Convention, and this time they decided to challenge the power of the Paris mob. To prove that they would not allow themselves to be treated as captives, they filed out of the Chamber. There they found themselves facing a solid line of Hanriot's soldiers, with thousands of civilians standing impassively behind them, watching the scene.

The deputies were led by the President of the Convention, Hérault de Séchelles. Quietly he walked up to where Hanriot, mounted on a great black charger, was prancing in front of his men.

"What do the people want?" inquired de Séchelles. "The Convention desires only their happiness."

E*

"The people have not risen to listen to empty talk," replied Hanriot contemptuously. "It demands that twenty-four guilty men shall be handed over to it."

"Hand us all over then," shouted a Girondin deputy.

All around the terrace outside the Convention chamber, men and women were beginning to scream and shake their fists.

"Purge the Convention," shouted one.

"Bleed it," yelled another. "To the guillotine with the Girondins."

The deputies, the elected representatives of the people of France, were helpless. They tried to find a way of escape but all around the chamber Hanriot's troops were drawn up in a solid ring. At one point Marat was waiting with a group of soldiers. Rushing forward toward his fellow deputies, he screamed : "I call upon you to return to the posts you have abandoned like cowards."

The deputies were not cowards. But what could they do? Confronted by the firmness of the National Guard and the hatred of the mob, they realized that anyone who resisted the wishes of the Jacobins was likely to find himself dragged off to prison and perhaps to the guillotine. So back they trooped into the chamber, there to listen to a triumphant and contemptuous speech by a Jacobin named Couthon, a fanatic and a cripple.

"All the members of the Convention," declared Couthon sarcastically, "can now feel sure they are free. I ask the Convention," he went on, "to decree that the twenty-two accused members be placed under arrest in their own homes."

Everyone in the chamber understood only too clearly what that meant. All the deputies remembered the prison massacres of the previous September, and they knew that arrest was likely to be only the first stage on the way to the guillotine.

"Pray give Couthon his glass of blood," a Girondin shouted. "He is thirsty."

But how many Girondins were supposed to be arrested? Twenty-two? Twenty-four? No one seemed certain; no one seemed to know exactly who was supposed to be on the list. Now Marat saw his chance to mock and torment his helpless enemies. Rising to his feet, he began to read out his own list of victims. First he read off one list of names, then went back to strike off one name and substitute another. Then, as if arguing with himself, he suggested yet another name, then another. While the Girondins whose fate he was deciding sat silent, he toyed with them like a cat with a mouse. When he finished, he had named twenty-nine Girondin deputies as traitors.

The voting was a mere formality. Without exception, all the Jacobins voted to expel and place under arrest the deputies on Marat's final list. Though a majority of the other deputies supported the Girondins, they sat silent. They were afraid that if they voted against the Jacobins, they would be seized by Hanriot's Guardsmen and sent to the guillotine. The insurrection had been a total success. Backed up by the Paris mob, the Jacobins had won a total victory. Now at last they controlled the legal government of France.

The Girondins who had been arrested included most of the men who had led the Revolution since the fall of 1791. There was Brissot, the former writer who had led France into war against the Austrians. There was Vergniaud, who had pronounced the sentence of death on Louis. There was Pétion who, as Mayor of Paris, had remained idle when the men from Marseilles stormed the Tuileries Palace, so as not to hinder the attack on the King. Roland could not be found; he, with a few other Girondin leaders, had escaped from Paris. Madame Roland was arrested in his place.

"Today a palace, tomorrow a prison," Madame Roland was to write later in her prison cell. "That is the righteous man's reward." To the end, the Girondins remained convinced that they had been right in trying to steer the Revolution along a moderate course. Certainly they had meant well and done what they believed to be best for France. But though the accusation that they were traitors was a vicious lie, perhaps they deserved to be driven from power. In time of revolution, a country needs strong, even ruthless men to lead it, and the Girondins were neither strong nor ruthless. Under their rule, France had tumbled into chaos. More revolts were breaking out in the provinces. The people of the cities had less food than ever. The army had been winning victories, yet its most distinguished general had deserted in despair. Now France was at war with England and Spain, Austria and Prussia. Young, unwilling boys were being dragged from their farms to serve as soldiers; while, at the front, the soldiers were almost starving and none of them seemed to know any longer what they were fighting for. Politicians are like major-league coaches; they must pay the price for failure. The Girondins had failed to inspire the people of France or to retain their trust. It was time for them to go. Yet as they were marched off as prisoners, many Frenchmen must surely have asked themselves: If these men are traitors, who have they betrayed? And if these men who were our heroes yesterday are our enemies today, how can anyone be trusted?

Throughout the debate in the Convention, Danton, the lion of the Revolution, had sat silent. He may not have liked the Girondins but still they had been his fellow ministers. Together, he and they had administered the government while France was being saved from the Prussian army. Less than a year before, when Marat had tried to get the Girondins arrested and executed, Danton, with a word, had been able to stop him. Now Marat had won. The Revolution was beginning to devour its own leaders. Perhaps Danton was wondering what would come next. Yet even he, for all his intelligence and ruthlessness, could not have anticipated the dreadful events that still lay ahead for the revolutionaries themselves, and for tens of thousands of ordinary French men and women who asked only to be left in peace.

CORDAY

# CHAPTER NINE

# ROBESPIERRE TAKES COMMAND

THE JACOBINS' success was not limited to Paris. In many towns throughout France, their agents had roused the mobs and, with their help, seized control of the local governments. But actually the Jacobins' situation was not as strong as it looked. For by the summer of 1793, so many revolts had broken out that all France was tottering on the brink of civil war.

One revolt took place in the port city of Bordeaux, in western France; another in Marseilles, the great French port on the Mediterranean; a third in Toulon, the biggest French naval base. Most important of all, a revolt also flared up against the Jacobin government in Lyons, the second largest city of France.

Why did these revolts take place? To some extent, they were the result of the war. It had now been dragging on for more than a year and most Frenchmen were heartily sick of it. The revolutionary armies had driven the invaders from the soil of France and few parents were willing to have their sons die merely to spread the Revolution to other countries. Because of the war, food was scarcer than ever; and prices kept going up so rapidly that in many towns the people were driven close to despair.

But the revolts were also a protest against the Jacobin extremists in Paris. In most towns the leading citizens had supported the Girondins, and they both hated and feared men like Marat and Robespierre. Moreover, the people in the provinces deeply resented the idea that they should have to obey a small group of fanatical, Parisian revolutionaries. If the people of Paris chose to be governed by the Jacobins and their hoodlum supporters, that was their business. But the citizens of Bordeaux and Toulon, Marseilles and Lyons did not see why they should be under the rule of extremists sent out to domineer them by the Jacobins of Paris.

The Jacobins therefore found themselves in a terrible predicament. To the north and east, they were facing the armies of Austria and Prussia. At sea, the British navy was sinking French ships and cutting off France's trade with other countries. Worst of all, to the south and west of Paris, the Jacobins were faced with armed revolts led by men who were determined to drive them from power.

It is doubtful whether the Jacobins could have kept control of the government if there had not taken place yet another of those extraordinary events which kept occurring throughout the Revolution. It was brought about by a girl of twenty-four named Charlotte Corday who lived in the small city of Caen on the north coast of France. Outwardly, she seemed to be a perfectly normal country girl. She was quiet and well mannered; good looking but not especially beautiful; intelligent yet not brilliant. She was, however, a girl of intense feelings. From her reading of books, she had come to hate the way the King and his aristocratic friends domi-

neered the ordinary men and women of France. The outbreak
of the Revolution, with all its talk of liberty and equality,
had thrilled her with joy. Her particular heroes were the
Girondins who believed in the principles of the Revolution,
yet hated brutality and violence. She came to look on them as
the saviors of France.

But gradually, like millions of other French men and
women, Charlotte Corday realized that something had gone
terribly wrong. The Revolution was supposed to bring peace
and justice and decency. But had it? Charlotte Corday heard
about the revolutionary soldiers who had come to a town
near her own and brutally beaten priests and other devout
Catholics who had refused to take the oath of loyalty. She
heard stories about the mobs of toughs and cutthroats running wild through the streets of Paris and attacking innocent citizens. Worst of all, she was horrified by the stories
which spread even to Caen of the savage massacres in the
Paris prisons.

Reading the newspaper published by Marat, Charlotte
decided — and quite rightly — that he was the man mainly
responsible for those massacres. She was outraged by the execution of the helpless Louis. Marat again. She was even
more deeply disturbed when she heard of the insurrection in
Paris that had led to the arrest of her heroes — the Girondins. Once again, she knew who was to blame. Marat. It was
Marat who kept spewing out his messages of hate and urging
the people on to further brutalities. Marat was the enemy of
all the things she believed in, more vicious and bloodthirsty
by far than the aristocrats had ever been in their days of
power. To Charlotte, Marat became the symbol of all the
hatred that had poisoned the Revolution and destroyed her

dream of a peaceful, happy France. Marat was a tyrant and Charlotte Corday, without telling anyone of her plans, decided to murder him.

On Tuesday, July 9, 1793, she took a seat in a stagecoach bound for Paris. Her plan was quite simple; she would go up to Marat in the middle of the Convention chamber and kill him where everyone could see. Then she would explain that she had struck him down as a warning to all the other fanatical Jacobins of the fate that awaited them unless they ceased their campaign of murder and terror.

When she reached Paris, Charlotte discovered that her plan could not work because Marat had not appeared in the Convention chamber since the day on which the Girondins had been expelled. His disappearance had nothing to do with politics. He had been forced to stay at home because the skin disease from which he suffered had spread all over his body and he could obtain relief only by sitting in a bath. There he spent almost all his time, squatting in a boot-shaped metal bathtub with a writing desk perched across it. With the desperate energy of the fanatic, he still drove himself to work, filling his newspaper with articles that urged his followers to continue their hunt for traitors and to kill them.

It was not hard for Charlotte to discover his address, and she quickly devised a new plan. She would murder Marat in his home. On the Saturday after she arrived in Paris, she went into a cutler's shop and picked out a long, sharp kitchen knife with an ebony handle that was easy to grasp. Back in her hotel room, she practiced hiding the knife under her clothes so that no one could see it. Then, with the knife safely concealed, she hired a carriage and drove to the house which Marat shared with three women. One was his sister. Another was a young woman named Simonne Evrard who, strange as it may seem, was in love with Marat. The third woman was Simonne's sister, Catherine.

The door was opened by Catherine Evrard who curtly told Charlotte that Marat was gravely ill and could see no one. But Charlotte was an extremely determined woman and this rebuff only led her to devise another plan that would enable her to get at the man she had resolved to kill.

In her home town of Caen, a group of Girondins had organized a revolt against the Jacobins. Charlotte knew that Marat, always eager to hear about traitors, would be glad to get any information she could give him about the revolt. Returning to her hotel, she wrote him a brief note: "I come from Caen. Your love for your country should make you curious to know about the plots that are taking place there. I will await your answer."

Charlotte had the note sent to Marat's house and settled down to wait for his reply. But several hours passed, no reply came, and Charlotte decided that she would make another attempt to gain admission to Marat's house. This time she managed to get inside the front door before being stopped by the woman who loved him, Simonne Evrard. An argument broke out. Charlotte insisted that she had vitally important information to give to Marat about the traitors in Caen and asked if he had received her note. Simonne insisted that he was too ill to see anybody. As they argued, their voices rose, and Marat overheard what Charlotte was saying. Actually, he had read her message and his curiosity had been aroused by it. Anxious to see what this visitor had to say, he ordered that she be allowed into his bathroom. A moment later Charlotte was standing there, looking down at the man she had come to kill.

He must have been a revolting sight. A towel soaked in

vinegar was twisted around his head, and the skin was peeling in long strips from his arms and shoulders. Still, though desperately sick, he was as eager as ever to obtain news about traitors, and he questioned Charlotte closely about the revolt in Caen. As Charlotte gave him the names of the ringleaders, he wrote them down, muttering with satisfaction: "Excellent. In a few days, I shall have them all guillotined."

The interview was over. Charlotte rose as if to leave. Then, suddenly, she stepped forward, pulled out her kitchen knife, and drove it into Marat's breast. He gave one brief cry for Simonne: "Help, dear friend. Help!" As Simonne Evrard dashed into the bathroom, Charlotte Corday walked calmly out. And she might very well have escaped had it not been for the presence in the sitting room of an assistant who was waiting to pick up an article Marat had been writing. Hearing the uproar and guessing that Marat had been attacked, this man grabbed a chair and brought it crashing down on Charlotte's head. She fell to the floor and Marat's assistant hurled himself on top of her. Before she could make any further attempt to escape, neighbors and police had rushed into the house, and she was dragged off to the Abbaye prison.

A few days later, she was brought to trial for the murder of Marat. Her guilt, of course, was obvious. It was her motive that puzzled the Jacobins.

"Why," the prosecutor asked her, "did you kill Marat? Who inspired you with so much hatred of him?"

"I didn't need the hatred of others," Charlotte answered calmly. "I had plenty of my own."

"But what did you hope to gain from killing him?"

"I killed one man to save a thousand."

"Do you think," asked the prosecutor sarcastically, "there was only one Marat?"

"No," said Charlotte. "But by killing him I have warned the others. His death will frighten the rest of them."

This, of course, was exactly the kind of reasoning which Marat himself had used. Kill a few traitors — or a few hundred or a few thousand — and the rest would abandon, out of fear, their attempts to betray the Revolution. But Charlotte's judgment was hopelessly wrong. In death Marat became even more of a hero to his followers than he had been in life. The people of Paris turned out in the thousands to watch his funeral procession. Young girls, dressed in white, the symbol of purity, walked beside the carriage in which Marat's shrunken body lay. Behind them marched the members of the Convention, followed by an enormous crowd of the sansculottes who had regarded Marat as their champion. As they marched, they shouted revolutionary slogans and sang patriotic songs while huge numbers of people fell on their knees as the procession passed by. "Oh, heart of Jesus," some chanted in prayer. "Oh, sacred heart of Marat."

Sacred heart of Marat! To his ardent followers, his death made him seem a saint, almost a god. His heart, cut from his body, was placed inside an urn that was suspended from the ceiling of the Cordeliers Club, one of the earliest and most famous meeting places of the Jacobins. There it stayed, like some religious relic, to remind his followers of all they owed him and to sustain their hatred against all the prosperous men and women who had been his enemies.

A few days later, Charlotte Corday was taken to her death on the guillotine. She made the journey in an open, heavy, lumbering, two-wheel farm cart. These carts, known as tumbrils, were soon to become a horribly familiar sight in Paris as they carried their human sacrifices to the guillotine. Because so many people wanted to see the murderess ride to her death, the tumbril that carried Charlotte Corday was taken over a long, roundabout route, winding in and out among the narrow streets. Huge crowds lined the route to catch a sight of this young and lovely murderess, and to spatter her with insults and curses. Convinced that she had struck a mighty blow for the true principles of the Revolution, Charlotte bore the insults with indifference. She remained calm until the end. The executioner, Sanson, was riding at her side and, as the tumbril turned to enter the Place de la Revolution, he placed himself between Charlotte and the guillotine so that she would not have to look at it. She asked him to move aside: "I have a right to be curious," she told him. "This is the first time I have ever seen one."

A few minutes later, the knife had fallen and the head of Charlotte Corday dropped into the basket. As had become the custom, one of the assistant executioners picked it up by the hair and swung it round so that the watching crowd could see it, and rejoice over the death of yet another enemy of the Revolution.

Had Charlotte Corday lived, she would very soon have realized that murdering Marat was to have precisely the opposite effect to that she had expected. She had hoped that his death would scare his fellow extremists and persuade them to stop massacring their political rivals. Actually, no single action could have provided Robespierre and the other Jacobins with a better excuse for wiping out all who tried to resist them. Few Jacobins believed Charlotte's story that the murder had been her own idea. A young, simple peasant girl come to Paris and, without telling anybody, murder so important a man as Marat! It seemed incredible. The murder, so the Jacobins argued, must have been part of a grand plot to destroy them. Charlotte Corday must certainly have had accomplices in planning it. And who were those accomplices? The Girondins, of course: the moderates, the prosperous members of the middle class, aided by priests and royalists and aristocrats. In fact, the people who had planned the murder of Marat represented the enemies of the Revolution who were rising in rebellion all over France to bring it to an end—according to the Jacobins.

Moreover, the murder of Marat had aroused his followers to a violent fury. He had been their hero. He had died a martyr to the cause of the Revolution, and the sansculottes of Paris and every other large city yearned to avenge his death. Perhaps it also scared many Jacobins into thinking that if they did not kill off their enemies first, then their enemies would kill them.

Thus Marat's death provided both the opportunity and the impetus for an all-out attack by the Jacobins on their enemies. Robespierre saw this more clearly than anyone. He realized that fear and the lust to avenge the murder of Marat had brought his followers to the point where they could be persuaded to massacre almost anyone who seemed to oppose them. Here was the chance to smash the revolts in Lyons and Marseilles and Toulon. Here was the chance to establish Jacobin rule with absolute authority: by arresting and executing (if necessary) their enemies, the moderates, in every town and village of France.

Only one obstacle stood in Robespierre's way. At the time of Marat's murder, Georges Danton was still the most popular and trusted man in France. A majority of the Convention would almost certainly have followed his lead. If he had wanted to fight Robespierre, Danton could probably have kept him from making himself the master of France. But

Danton was weary. For more than a year, he had driven himself with relentless energy to make the Revolution secure. Now he believed that it had gone far enough and that there had already been too much blood shed in France. He had grown tired of the incessant struggles and intrigues for power. He was sick of the constant cry that anyone who disagreed with the Jacobins was a traitor, an enemy of the Revolution. He was sick of the sight of Frenchmen killing each other. Above all, Danton was convinced that France should end her war against Austria and Prussia, England and Spain. The invaders had long since been cleared from French soil. On his many visits to the front, Danton had witnessed the terrible sufferings of the revolutionary soldiers. So far as he could see, continuing the war would simply mean more suffering: more shortages of food at home and more deaths — useless deaths — on the battlefield.

Feeling as he did, Danton had begun secretly to try to make peace with France's foreign enemies. But the war seemed to have taken on a momentum of its own. Now that they controlled the French government, most of the Jacobins had become more determined than ever to crush the foreign governments of kings and emperors and aristocrats, and they strongly disapproved of Danton's efforts to end the war.

Thus Danton found himself in conflict with the very people who had once been his closest friends. Tired of bloodshed, sickened by the never-ending cries of treason, he became disgusted with the political struggle that was raging in Paris. He also had another and much more personal reason for wanting to retreat from the political battle. Just after Marat was murdered, he had married again, this time a girl of sixteen. He had always enjoyed the peace and quiet of his home and garden, and he now decided that he would rather spend his time with his young wife than arguing in the Convention in Paris. So, gradually, Danton began to spend less and less of his time in Paris, leaving the way open for Robespierre to take command.

Under Robespierre's vigorous leadership, the Jacobins determined to ensure their power by the simple method of arresting and, if necessary, killing off, their opponents. To achieve this end, the Convention passed what became known as the Law of Suspects. According to this law, anyone was liable to arrest if he had shown himself to be a "supporter of tyranny" or an "enemy of liberty." In fact, anyone was suspect if he had not "constantly demonstrated his support of the Revolution."

These words were deliberately vague. What they really meant was that anyone was a suspected traitor if the Jacobins said he was. The Law of Suspects went even further. It set up local vigilance committees in every city and village whose job was to hand out "certificates of good citizenship." Anyone who could not obtain a certificate was automatically assumed to be a bad citizen; or, in other words, an enemy of the Revolution. Naturally the members of the vigilance committees were all ardent Jacobins. So anyone who aroused the displeasure of the Jacobins in his district was liable to be arrested and imprisoned.

Under this law, France became a country ruled by terror. The atmosphere of terror grew and grew until no citizen, however innocent, could feel safe from the threat of the guillotine.

One of the first victims was the former Queen, Marie Antoinette. Through all the upheavals of the Revolution, the Jacobins had never forgotten their hatred of her, and, since the execution of her husband, they had treated her cruelly.

First her children were taken from her, to be brought up by
sansculottes jailers. Then, about a month after the death of
Marat, she was moved to a cell where she was kept in solitary
confinement. Her cell was in the Conciergerie prison which
occupied the bottom floor of a building called the Palace of
Justice. Actually it was a death house. There, as everyone
was soon to learn, prisoners were taken to spend the last
days of their lives before they were summoned to trial and
condemned to die under the guillotine.

Throughout the early fall of 1793, the Conciergerie began to
fill up as men and women were rounded up under the Law of
Suspects. Most of them were heaped together in a long stone
corridor that was known as the Mousetrap. In this narrow
corridor, hundreds of prisoners lay or squatted on filthy mat-
tresses. They were packed so close together that there was no
room to step by, and any prisoner wanting to walk along the
corridor had to tread on the bodies of his fellow prisoners.

On either side of the Mousetrap were dozens of little cells,
divided from each other by thin, wooden partitions. These
were the cells where prisoners who had money could buy
themselves a shred of privacy. In one, Madame Roland
passed her last weeks, writing her memoirs and being visited
by her old Girondin friends and fellow prisoners. They at
least were allowed to take some exercise in the tiny prison
courtyard. Marie Antoinette was treated more viciously. She
was kept inside her small square stone cell. Its single barred
window formed her only contact with the outside world, and
through it, all she could see were the legs of the women
prisoners as they walked around the courtyard. She was not
allowed even a candle to read by. When darkness fell, the
only light in her cell came from a dim oil lamp that flickered
in the passage outside. Cold struck upward from the damp,

stone floor. Four years before, she had been surrounded by courtiers and ladies-in-waiting while servants — footmen and maids and hairdressers and cooks — stood ready to obey her slightest whim. Now she was waited on only by a young girl who came in to clean her cell and bring her food. And, on the further side of a wooden screen which stretched across the cell, two guards remained constantly on watch in case any attempt should be made to rescue her.

Once, Marie Antoinette had bought three hundred magnificent gowns a year; now she was not even allowed a needle to patch up her single shabby prison dress. She had nothing to help her while away the dark, solitary hours. In this ghastly brutal solitude, her health gradually failed. She lost the sight of one eye. Because of some internal disease, she began to bleed steadily. A surgeon who was brought to treat her could do nothing. Not that it would have made much difference if he had been able to, for Marie Antoinette was soon to face trial on the charge of treason.

The court which tried her was known as the Revolutionary Tribunal. The Tribunal had been set up a few months before, at Danton's suggestion. His intention was to prevent any more massacres like the ones that had occurred in the prisons of Paris. Instead of being butchered by any group of blood-thirsty street toughs, suspected enemies of the Revolution would be brought before the Tribunal and there they would receive a fair trial.

That had been Danton's plan. Actually, matters turned out very differently. For the Revolutionary Tribunal was under the control of the National Convention, and when Robespierre and his supporters became masters of the Convention, the Tribunal lay ready to their hand. It suited them perfectly. Now they no longer needed to butcher their enemies in the prisons and the streets. They could have the people they disliked brought up before the Tribunal and, under the pretense of giving them a fair trial, have them legally condemned to death.

Outwardly, the Tribunal did seem to give its victims a fair trial. It met in a long, bare room on the second floor of the Palace of Justice, directly above the cells of the Conciergerie prison. At one end of the room, the panel of judges sat on a raised platform. Their job, officially, was to see that the trial was conducted fairly. To one side, sat the members of the jury, who were supposed to consider the evidence and decide whether the accused were innocent or guilty. But the judges were not the kind of men we think of when we hear the word "judge." They had no training in the law and no duty to conduct fair trials. They and the members of the jury were picked by the Convention, and both judges and jurors knew that their job was simply to find all accused prisoners guilty and condemn them to death.

The most important member of the Tribunal was the Public Prosecutor, Fouquier-Tinville. He was yet another of the bloodthirsty fanatics who rose to power during the Revolution. It was Fouquier-Tinville, from his seat just below the judges' dais, who actually ran the Tribunal. He was in his late forties, a man with thick dark hair and heavy eyebrows over small, piercing eyes. His normal expression was a threatening scowl. He was quick, decisive, brilliant, and enormously industrious. Aided by a group of obedient assistants, he worked with tremendous energy to dig up every scrap of evidence he could find against the accused who were brought before him. He was not interested in justice. There was not a scrap of mercy in his body. In fact he was rather like a machine, a kind of human computer who absorbed all the rumors and accusations to be found against his victims, hurled them at the judges and the jury, and then issued his demands for death.

It was against this man that Marie Antoinette was summoned for trial on October the fifteenth, 1793. Busy as he was, Fouquier-Tinville had dredged up all the evidence he could find to show that she was a traitor. That day, the galleries of the courtroom were packed with spectators, most of them sluts and fishwives from the Paris slums. They had come to mock and to sneer at the hated former Queen. But when she appeared at last in the courtroom, leaning for support on the arm of an officer, the women fell silent. They could hardly believe that this poor, broken woman was the haughty, beautiful, arrogant Marie Antoinette they had once envied and hated. She was indeed barely recognizable. The skin had crumbled over her wasted cheeks and, because of her long illness, her once lovely figure had become almost that of a skeleton. Still, she retained something of her old majesty. Indeed suffering seemed to have given her a new kind of dignity. She must have resolved that if she was to die, she would die bravely. Louis, at his trial, had been given an armchair to sit in. For Marie Antoinette, there was only a hard wooden bench. On it, she sat calmly, showing no sign of fear as she gazed across at Fouquier-Tinville who faced her.

Fouquier-Tinville had done all he could to make a strong case. One after another, he called the witnesses — forty-one of them — to describe in detail all the treasonous acts of the former Queen. She had wasted the people's money with her extravagances at Versailles. She had inspired loyal soldiers of the French army with hatred for the Revolution. She had urged the King to resist the loyal revolutionaries — including the cutthroats from Marseilles who had stormed the Tuileries Palace . . .

On and on went Fouquier-Tinville, rasping out the old, familiar accusations. Marie Antoinette had planned the escape that was stopped at Varennes. She had urged her brother, the Emperor of Austria, to invade France and overthrow the Revolution. She had given the Austrians secret information about the French army. These charges were all true; the documents which prove they were true have since been found. But Fouquier-Tinville himself had not been able to find any of that evidence. Putting on a tremendous display of indignation, he covered the table which stood before the judges with one article after another; locks of hair cut from Marie Antoinette and her children, an old portrait of the Princesse de Lamballe, lists of names of the former Queen's servants . . . But he did not produce a single document in Marie Antoinette's writing that would prove her to be guilty of the accusations he hurled against her.

Hour after hour, the trial dragged on; for fifteen hours on the first day, for twelve more on the second. Still Marie Antoinette managed to retain her calm and her dignity. At last Fouquier-Tinville finished presenting the case for the prosecution, and Marie Antoinette was asked if she had anything further to say.

"No one," she answered, "has brought forward any positive charge. I have therefore nothing to say except that I was only the wife of Louis the Sixteenth and that I had to comply with his wishes."

Silence. Fouquier-Tinville summed up the charges, and the jury retired to another room to consider their verdict.

They stayed out a long time. One hour passed, then an-

other, and Marie Antoinette began to hope that perhaps she
would not be sentenced to death. Perhaps she would only be
banished from France and left to live out her life in peace.
The hope was a vain one. Both the judges and the jurors
knew that if the former Queen were not condemned to die,
they themselves might be sent to the guillotine as traitors to
the Revolution. When they finally returned to their seats, the
jurors announced that they had found Marie Antoinette
guilty of treason. She was brought back from her cell, so exhausted that she could hardly stand, to hear her sentence.
Fouquier-Tinville demanded the death penalty; the judges
agreed, and Marie Antoinette was led back down the spiral
staircase to her cell.

On the dark stairway, her eyesight failed for a moment,
she missed a step, and almost fell. The officer who was escorting her offered her his arm. During the trial he had brought
her a glass of water. For having committed these "crimes,"
he was solemnly accused of "treason," and barely escaped
being sent to the guillotine.

Marie Antoinette was to die on the next day. Most of that
night she sat up, writing a farewell letter to her sister-in-law,
Madame Elisabeth. At five in the morning, while she was still
at her desk, drummers all over Paris began to pound out the
funereal roll that accompanied every execution. By seven,
the armed forces of the capital were at their posts. Foot soldiers lined the sidewalks, while groups of cavalry were
massed at strategic points ready to race to the scene in case
any attempt were made to save the former Queen.

For more than a year Marie Antoinette had not been out in
the open air. Carefully, she smoothed her white gown,
wrapped her neck in a muslin cloth and put on her one good
pair of shoes. She covered her hair, now snow white, with a

two-winged cap. Outside the exit from the Conciergerie prison a tumbril was drawn up and waiting. Louis had ridden to his death in a closed carriage but since then the Revolution had taken many steps forward. Now all men and women were supposed to be equal, and so Marie Antoinette had to ride to the guillotine, standing in an open farm cart, like all other condemned prisoners.

However, the lines of soldiers and the crowds that gathered behind them showed that the people of Paris regarded this as no ordinary execution. In huge numbers they had turned out to taste their final revenge on the woman who had once been the very symbol of aristocratic tyranny. Here and there, groups of women shouted insults at her while at one point an actor in the uniform of a National Guardsman swung in close to her cart, waving his sword and shouting: "There she is, the infamous Marie Antoinette. She's done for at last, my friends."

Marie Antoinette seemed not to hear. Perhaps her thoughts were too far away. Perhaps she was simply determined not to give her enemies the satisfaction of showing that she noticed their jeers. As if oblivious of the crowds, she stared straight ahead, while the drums continued their unceasing beat and the tumbril slowly lumbered through the streets to the open space where the uprights of the guillotine towered stark against the sky.

There was a stir among the vast crowd which thronged the Place de la Revolution, and murmurs of "Here she comes." A squadron of cavalry clattered into the square, then, behind them, the cart bearing the former Queen. Now suddenly the drummers stopped their beat and a silence fell. It was so still that the stamp of the horses and the rumble of wheels was clearly audible as the tumbril drew up beside the guillotine.

Sanson, the executioner, sprang down from the cart and, walking beside him, Marie Antoinette slowly mounted the steps to the platform. Without a word, she removed her scarf and bonnet. Sanson thrust her body down on the wooden slab and arranged her head inside the wooden vice. He pulled the string, the knife of the guillotine flashed downward, and the head of Marie Antoinette fell into the basket.

Within a few minutes, the huge square was almost empty. The spectators had scattered to go back to their daily business and the body of Marie Antoinette was wheeled away in a little handcart, the head crushed down between the legs.

That day Hébert, the journalist of hate, wrote triumphantly in his newspaper:

"If only I could convey to you the delight of the sansculottes when the arch tigress was driven across Paris in the tumbril . . At long last her accursed head was severed from her neck and the air resounded to cries of 'Long Live the Republic.' "

But Hébert's report was false. There had been little delight in Paris that day. Though a few fanatical Jacobins had exulted over the sight of Marie Antoinette riding to her death, most of the crowd had watched the procession in silence. Perhaps the sight of a defenseless woman riding calmly to the guillotine had made them ashamed. Indeed, the execution of Marie Antoinette was a thoroughly meaningless act. As Queen, she had been the most famous woman in Europe. Now, in death, she was no more significant than any other victim of the Revolution. In her cell at the Conciergerie, a warder gathered up the few scraps of clothing she had left and sent them to a hospital, unmarked so that no one who wore them would know from whom they had been taken. And an undertaker submitted his bill: "Widow Capet, for the

F

coffin, six livres. For a grave and the gravediggers, fifteen livres." The price was a low one, for the revolutionaries were not prepared to show any special favors to the dead body of a Queen. A single funeral was expensive. Why should the people pay for it? So the body of Marie Antoinette was kept in a mortuary until three score other "traitors" had been executed, and then was tossed with their bodies into a common grave.

Shortly before Marie Antoinette was sent to the guillotine the former leaders of the Girondins were also brought to trial before the Revolutionary Tribunal. It was inevitable that they should have been among Fouquier-Tinville's first victims. Robespierre and his supporters were determined to justify the harshness of the actions which they were taking against everyone who might oppose them. If they were to retain the support of enough Frenchmen to keep themselves in power, they believed that they must prove that their enemies really were traitors to the Revolution.

This kind of political trial occurs frequently in history when a group of politicians seize absolute power and make themselves dictators. As dictators, they permit no opposition. But there are always some people, perhaps many, who resent losing their freedom. The dictators therefore face a difficult problem. Somehow they must justify the iron grip they impose on the people. The method they usually adopt is to try to prove that dictatorship is necessary for the good of the nation. They assert, just as the Jacobins did, that their enemies are really traitors. They talk of plots and intrigues. To back up their talk, they hold political trials which are carefully planned to prove that their victims are enemies of the nation. The Nazis did the same when they seized power in Germany in the 1930's. The Communists did the same when they made themselves the rulers of Russia. The same process is still going on: Whenever a revolution occurs, and a new group of rulers seize power, they are liable to charge their enemies with treason. It was the Jacobins who introduced this method of justifying a dictatorship and this is one of the many reasons that make the French Revolution so important an event in history. Today, nearly two hundred years later, fanatical politicians are still copying the methods used by Robespierre and his followers. They are still using exactly the same words and telling the same kinds of lies in an attempt to fool their peoples and secure their own power.

By bringing the Girondins to trial, Robespierre hoped to rally the people of France more firmly behind him. But he was taking a grave risk. It was easy for the Revolutionary Tribunal to condemn Marie Antoinette. She had opposed the Revolution from the beginning. Moreover, she was a weak and desperately ill woman, barely able to speak up in her own defense. The Girondins were quite a different proposition. They were lawyers, orators, politicians used to argument, and they had once commanded the support of enough Frenchmen to make them the strongest political party in France.

It was, of course, easy for the Jacobins just to say that these men had shown themselves to be traitors to the Revolution. But to make such arguments sound convincing in a courtroom was much harder. Still, Fouquier-Tinville did his best. In his cold, metallic voice, he repeated all the accusations that Marat and Robespierre had for so long been making against the Girondins. They had engaged in secret plots with Louis, the former king. They had led France into war. They had been friends and allies of the traitorous general,

Dumouriez. They had tried to crush the people of Paris. They had condemned that glorious revolutionary act of the previous September: the prison massacres. That surely proved they were really friends of the aristocrats and priests who had been killed. Moreover, they had tried to save Louis from execution as a tyrant and a traitor.

The Girondins knew that the Tribunal was bound to find them guilty. They knew they would be sent to the guillotine. But they were determined to go down fighting and they boldly answered Fouquier-Tinville's charges. It was true, they conceded, that they had tried to cooperate with Louis. But then, by doing so, they had only been following the principles set up by the revolutionary constitution. It was true that they had led France into war; but they had done it to unite France behind the Revolution. And, as they pointed out, the Jacobins were still fighting that same war against the same foreign enemies. It was true that they had opposed the wishes of the Paris mob; but they had done so because as representatives of all France, they had thought it wrong that the government should be at the mercy of street mobs. It was true that they had once been friends of Dumouriez; but it was to overthrow them that Dumouriez had planned to march his army on Paris. And as for the accusation that they had tried to save Louis's life . . . had not almost all of them voted for his execution?

So, point by point, the Girondins countered every one of Fouquier-Tinville's accusations, and, as the argument proceeded, they began to get the upper hand. Gradually, a sense of uneasiness spread throughout the courtroom. The spectators who packed the galleries were all ardent Jacobins but even they began to suffer doubts as they listened to the impassioned defense of the Girondins. These men, after all, had led the Revolution for more than a year. How then could they be considered its enemies?

As the arguments raged on, Fouquier-Tinville observed doubt growing among the spectators, and he became frightened. The trial was not proceeding as he had planned. Instead of showing up the Girondins as traitors, it was making them look like men unjustly accused. Somehow the trial had to be ended and the Girondins silenced.

In his fear, Fouquier-Tinville turned to the Convention for help. "It is now five days," he reported, "since the trial began, and only nine witnesses have been heard. The accused answer the witnesses, and are answered back. So a debate starts which is as long as the speakers are talkative. At this rate, the trial will never end." And why, he went on to ask, need there be any witnesses at all, when everyone knows that the accused are guilty?

Either from belief or from fear, all the deputies who still remained in the Convention were supporters of the Jacobins. They, too, could see that the Girondins were arousing sympathy. They shared Fouquier-Tinville's fears. Hurriedly, they passed a decree, stating that a trial might end at any time after three days if the jurors had heard enough evidence to make up their minds.

The jurors took the hint. As soon as the decree was read out, they declared that they had heard enough, and the trial could now be ended. As if to show that they had been considering their verdict with care, the jurors stayed out for three hours. Then they filed back into their seats and declared that all the accused were guilty.

Inevitably, Fouquier-Tinville demanded the death sentence, and the judges hastened to deliver it. But unlike most other victims, the Girondins did not accept the sentence calmly. They rose to their feet, waved their arms, and shouted that the trial had been unfair. It had not even been conducted according to the Tribunal's own rules. "I die," shouted one Girondin, pointing to the judges, "on the day that the people lost their reason; you, you will die on the day that they find it again."

During this uproar, one of the Girondins, Valazé, was seen to stagger and Vergniaud, who was standing beside him, asked: "What is the matter? Are you frightened?"

"I am dying," Valazé answered and he collapsed on the floor at Vergniaud's feet. To escape the guillotine, he had stabbed himself to death. From Fouquier-Tinville's reaction, we can get a clear idea of the man's crazy fanaticism. He was so enraged that one of his victims should escape a public execution that he demanded that the corpse of Valazé be taken to the guillotine to be beheaded. Though frightened lackeys of the Convention, the judges could not bring themselves to order the beheading of a corpse. Instead, they decided on a compromise. The body of the dead man should be carried on a tumbril with his comrades to the Place de la Revolution, and then, after the executions, be buried with them in a common grave.

Two weeks after the execution of Marie Antoinette, the Girondins followed her to the guillotine. They went to their deaths bravely, waving to the crowds as they passed. As they stood on the platform, waiting for their turn to die, they sang the great hymn of the Revolution, the *"Marseillaise,"* the sound of their voices growing steadily weaker as, one by one, they were seized and thrust under the guillotine.

Next it was the turn of Madame Roland. She was brought

before the Revolutionary Tribunal in place of her husband who had not yet been captured. Months before she had seen the direction that the Revolution was taking.

"The time will come," she wrote in her prison cell, "when the people will ask for bread and be given corpses." In front of the Tribunal, she made no effort to defend herself. Instead she spoke in praise of her old, murdered friends. The judges stopped her, declaring that was "praising crimes." Her trial was quickly over; the sentence, death.

Cool, calm, and smiling, Madame Roland rode to her death past mobs of shouting, cursing sansculottes. Beside the guillotine, a statue, intended to represent the spirit of liberty, had been built on a pedestal which once had supported a statue of King Louis the Fifteenth. The figure was that of a woman, holding in her hand the sword of justice. As she stood on the platform beside the guillotine, the eyes of Madame Roland fell on the statue. "Oh, liberty," she murmured. "What crimes are committed in thy name." A moment later, and she, too, was dead.

There still remained several Girondin leaders who had managed to escape from Paris. Inexorably, they were hunted down. One was dragged to the guillotine in the city of Bordeaux. Two others blew out their brains in a forest where they had been hiding, and their bodies were found, half-eaten by wild dogs. Another shot himself in prison before he could be executed. Yet another took poison.

And what of Roland, that pompous, conceited incompetent, who had once believed that he could make himself the most powerful man in France? "When my husband hears of my death," Madame Roland had prophesied, "he will kill himself." She proved to be right. Hiding in the city of Rouen, Roland heard a newsboy in the street, calling out the news of his wife's execution. It was a cold night, lit brightly by the moon. Without a word to anyone, the brokenhearted Roland walked off into a forest, and there shot himself. Beside his body, he left a note: "Whoever thou art that findeth me lying here, respect my remains. They are those of a man who died as he had lived, in virtue and honesty."

But there was now no place left in France for virtue or for honesty. Liberty, Equality, and Fraternity: that had been the rallying cry of the men who brought about the Revolution. They had dreamed of a France in which every citizen would be his own master, free from tyranny and equal before the law. Instead, the Revolution had been taken over by the Jacobins. And they, for all their fine talk about liberty and equality, were proving themselves to be more ruthless and tyrannical than the worst of the hated aristocrats.

Danton, the man who had saved the Revolution, saw clearly what was happening. He was in his house in the country when a friend rushed into the garden, bearing the news that the Girondins had been executed. In his rage and his despair, Danton cried out: "We all deserve to be guillotined as much as they. We will all of us share their fate one after the other. These men in Paris will guillotine the whole Republic."

Even as he spoke, the men in Paris were plotting their next moves against the "enemies of the Revolution." Under their guidance, a kind of madness was to descend over France. "Give Couthon his glass of blood," a Girondin deputy had shouted in the Convention four months earlier. "He is thirsty." Soon all France was to learn how thirsty the Jacobins could be. Blood, blood and yet more blood was to be their battle cry. They were about to plunge their country into a period of such ghastly horror that it has become known in history simply as the Terror.

F*

Raffet del.                                                    Bosselman sc.

ST. JUST

# CHAPTER TEN

# THE COMMITTEE OF PUBLIC SAFETY

---

ALL THROUGH the fall of 1793, and throughout the winter and spring to come, an observer would have noticed an intense bustle inside the Tuileries Palace. This building, which had once housed King Louis and his Queen, had now become the headquarters of the revolutionary government. In the corridors, minor clerks, secretaries and errand boys jostled up against high-ranking army officers and deputies of the Convention. Occasionally, a courier from one of the provinces would come hurrying in, the mud still clinging to his boots. Impatiently, he would push his way through the crowds of officials to a door where two sentries stood guard twenty-four hours a day. Entrance through that door was difficult. Only people with extremely urgent business were allowed through it. For behind the door, gathered around a large oval table covered with a green cloth sat the members of the Committee of Public Safety — the men who now ruled France.

The Committee had been set up by Danton a few months before the Jacobins seized power. His idea was that it should act as an executive body to control the various departments of government, such as the army, the navy, and the treasury.

According to Danton's plan, the elected deputies who sat in the Convention would remain the real rulers of France. The members of the Committee would be elected by the deputies and changed regularly, and they would simply carry out the everyday work of running the government.

In July, however, Danton left the Committee. A few weeks later, Robespierre joined it. From that moment on, the Committee established itself as all-powerful. In theory, it had to obey the Convention. In practice, it was master. For as a member of the Committee, Robespierre kept on using the same technique he had used against the Girondins. Anyone who opposed him was accused of being a traitor to the Revolution, and was liable to be executed. Now that he was the strongest member of the government, Robespierre was more dangerous than ever. And in their fear of him, the deputies approved every suggestion the Committee made.

Not that Robespierre had matters all his own way. There were twelve members of the Committee and, officially, they were all equal. A majority of them had to agree before any important decisions were taken. Because their discussions were secret, we do not know what their disagreements were. The members of the Committee kept their quarrels to themselves. They had learned their lesson from watching the Girondins. They would not let their opponents divide them. Nor would they allow personal feelings and friendships to interfere with their efficiency.

Under the incompetent Girondins, the whole of France had drifted into chaos. Some of the largest French cities were in a state of rebellion against the government. Looking around them, the members of the Committee of Public Safety realized that they would have to be completely ruthless to re-establish order. What is more, they determined to crush the rebels in such a way that no one would dare to rebel again.

So the Terror began. Historians still disagree on exactly where and when it came into being. But one of the first places it struck was Lyons, the great industrial center, where supporters of the Girondins had taken over the city government. These men were determined not to submit to the Jacobins in Paris and they put up a fierce resistance against the army which the Committee of Public Safety sent to crush them. But the commander of that army was General Kellermann, one of the generals who had commanded the French soldiers at the vital battle of Valmy. He was a skillful and ruthless man. For several weeks he besieged the city while his cannons fired a steady stream of cannonballs against it. Finally, the defenders ran so short of food that they were forced to give in.

Now the Jacobins had their chance to punish the rebels and they did so with quite remarkable brutality. Lyons, they decided, must be destroyed. Its buildings were to be torn down, stone by stone. The very name of Lyons was to be struck off the map and a column was to be built among the ruins, bearing the words: "Lyons made war on liberty. Lyons no longer exists."

To take charge of this operation, the Committee sent one of its own members, the cripple, Couthon. Unable to walk, he was carried through the streets of the beaten city in a chair, and, from it, he pointed out the houses he wanted destroyed. In particular, he concentrated on the houses which belonged to the wealthiest citizens. As soon as he had passed on, gangs of workmen went to work, tearing the houses down.

Within a few weeks, whole areas of Lyons had been turned into a mass of rubble. But still the members of the Committee of Public Safety in Paris were not satisfied. Couthon was not ruthless enough for them, so they sent down another member of the Committee named Collot d'Herbois to take his place. He was one of the most brutal men in France and soon he had special tribunals working overtime to "try" the rebels. But the trials were a farce. The rebels were brought up in front of the tribunals in batches; they were hardly given a chance to defend themselves before they were condemned to death. In fact, the guillotine in Lyons could not work fast enough to kill off Collot's victims. So he ordered many to be put up against a wall and shot. Then, to speed the executions further, he had two hundred men and women taken out into a field, bound together, and mowed down with cannonballs.

Soon afterwards, the rebellion in the port city of Marseilles was also crushed. There, too, Jacobins arrived from Paris to punish the rebels. Once more tribunals were set up and the "enemies of the Revolution" were tried and condemned by the hundred. Then it was the turn of Toulon, the main French naval base. Under the watchful eye of the Paris agents, twelve thousand workmen went to work to pull down all the finest houses in the city. While that was being done, the rebels were being relentlessly hunted down and executed. And soon the chief Jacobin was able to report to the Convention: "Every day since our arrival, two hundred citizens of Toulon have been shot."

Of all the terrorists, a man called Carrier was the worst. He was given the job of punishing the rebels in the port city of Nantes. Carrier was a former army officer who sometimes suffered from fits in which he would fall to the floor, howling like a dog. He was a maniac, and the massacres he ordered were even worse than those that had taken place in the prisons of Paris a year before. In fact, Carrier did not even bother to pretend that he was just killing people who had resisted the Jacobins. One day he had five hundred young boys and girls taken out into a field to be clubbed and shot to death. Then he had another idea. Hundreds of people were seized by his soldiers; rich citizens and poor ones, businessmen and peasants, young boys and girls, mothers with young babies in their arms . . . anyone in Nantes was liable to be taken. They were then herded together onto rafts which were pushed out into the middle of the river that flowed past the city. Once the rafts were in midstream, the plugs were pulled out and the rafts sank, drowning everyone on board.

No one knows how many people died as a result of the revenge which the Jacobin terrorists took on the cities that had risen in rebellion against them. Carrier alone must have massacred several thousand. It took years for the cities of Lyons and Marseilles and Toulon to recover from the terrible destruction. These mass executions and the tearing down of houses might seem the work of madmen, and it is true that some terrorists, such as Carrier, truly were mad. But many of the terrorists were not at all mad. Men like Couthon and Collot d'Herbois were certainly very brutal. But they, and their fellow members of the Committee of Public Safety, knew exactly what they were doing. Their policy was to show the people of France that rebellion against the government meant death. Therefore it would be best for everybody to obey the Jacobins. This was the message behind the Terror, and it worked. So long as the Jacobins remained in power, no one else dared to rebel against them.

Under the rule of the Committee of Public Safety, France became what is now called a police state. The people were no longer free. In every city, Jacobins took over control of the local government. In every section of every city, local vigilance committees were set up. The men who served on these committees were street toughs — rough, idle bullies who reveled in their new power. Badly dressed, dirty, often drunk, these men treated their fellow Frenchmen with open contempt, and they were particularly vicious to anyone who looked or talked like a lady or gentleman. Yet no one who valued his life dared to complain. For the slightest sign of resistance was enough to damn a man as an "enemy of the people." And anyone who was accused of being an enemy of the people would either be thrown in jail or be dragged in front of the Revolutionary Tribunal which would probably order him to be guillotined.

Still, all this was only one side of the Jacobins' rule. Brutal and vicious as they were, the members of the Committee of Public Safety were also extremely hard-working and efficient. A majority of them were extreme Jacobin revolutionaries. Couthon was such a man. So were Collot d'Herbois and his friend Billaud-Varenne. They were both loud, self-assertive bullies, and, like most bullies, they were also cowards. Another of the Jacobin politicians, St. Just, was quite different. He was tall, young, elegant and extremely handsome. Although he was a revolutionary, he dressed as elegantly as any nobleman, and he was also as haughty as any of the aristocrats he hated. St. Just hero-worshipped Robespierre. It was one of his few passions. Normally he was as icy and bloodless as a machine, and because he was so cold-blooded and yet so handsome, he was given the nickname : the Archangel of Death.

All these men, like Robespierre himself, were politicians. They had come to power because they were leaders of the Jacobin party. The other members of the Committee were not so much politicians as practical, hardheaded administrators; the kind of men who today would be executives in large corporations. Carnot, who was in charge of the army, was one such man. Lindet, whose job was to reorganize France's farms and factories, was another. These executives went along with the Terror because they thought it was necessary to rescue France from chaos. But their main interest was in running their departments in the government.

Different though they were, the terrorists, like Robespierre or Collot d'Herbois or Couthon, and the administrators, like Carnot and Lindet, managed to work together in harmony. With amazing speed, they imposed an iron grip on France. They picked out competent officials and sent them wherever there was trouble. These officials were known as representatives on mission, and they carried papers which gave them authority to act with all the powers of the Committee itself. They set up local governments and chose the men to run them. They also wrote enormously long and detailed reports which were carried back at top speed by couriers to the Committee in Paris.

From these reports, the Committee was able to see what needed to be done to make the country efficient. No detail seemed too trivial for their attention and they acted always with extraordinary speed and decision. Suppose a group of farmers were refusing to send their produce to the nearby town. Very soon officials or soldiers would arrive to persuade them to change their minds. A factory perhaps was not producing as much ammunition as it was supposed to. The manager would be fired and somebody more competent would be appointed in his place. Was a regiment short of boots? Was a ship stuck in port because new sails had not been made? The

Committee would send out agents to find out why, and quickly the failure would be corrected.

Under the rule of the Committee, tens of thousands of Frenchmen found that they were better off than they had ever been before. This was especially true in the cities. Most of the working people found that they had more food to eat and better clothes to wear. And there were plenty of jobs, turning out supplies for the armies. In fact, there was more work than there were workers to do it. For the army was growing at tremendous speed and with every week that passed it became more formidable.

In the summer of 1793, when the Jacobins seized power, the position of the French army seemed desperate. Every nation in Western Europe had joined in the Alliance to crush the revolutionary government. Spain and England, Austria, Prussia and Holland, all were at war with France. Their soldiers stood poised once again along the frontiers, facing the feeble French armies. Their navies had driven the French ships from the seas. It looked as if the Revolution was bound to be crushed; and then the émigré nobles would at long last return to take their revenge.

That summer, the Committee of Public Safety decided on a daring plan. Up until the time of the French Revolution, most armies were quite small. The soldiers were either peasants dragged at random from their fields; or else they were professional soldiers who would fight for anyone who paid them. It was the French revolutionaries who first thought of organizing what is now called the draft.

"From this moment," declared the Committee of Public Safety, "until that when the enemy is driven from the territory of the republic, every Frenchman is commandeered for the needs of the armies. Young men will go to the front.

Married men will forge arms and carry food; women will make tents and clothing, and work in hospitals; children will turn old linen into bandages."

Thus, everyone was to be mobilized to fight off the invaders. But could such a plan work? Many people thought it impossible. The whole French nation, they said, is utterly weary of the war and longs only for peace. But actually the Committee of Public Safety had hit on a wonderful idea. It had called on the desire for equality which had led to the Revolution. If *all* the young men had to join the army and *all* the women had to go to work making supplies, then everyone would be treated equally. No one would be getting special treatment.

Inspired by this appeal to the principles of the Revolution, the French rallied to the Committee's call to arms. With surprisingly little grumbling, the whole French nation buckled down to the task of winning the war. Now the brutal efficiency of the Committee of Public Safety produced its most telling results. The navy, the army, the factories that turned out weapons and ammunition — all were reorganized. Everywhere, the Committee's agents were at work, inspecting, asking questions, making fresh plans. In and out of Paris they galloped along the dusty highways, carrying their reports to the Tuileries Palace, and returning with new instructions.

Soon newly formed regiments were marching off to the front, better equipped than they had ever been before. Meanwhile, the Committee was also doing its best to see that the soldiers would have the best generals to lead them. A personal representative of the Committee sat beside every general as he made his plans, and galloped at his side, as he led his men into battle. These representatives also sent back reports to Paris. If a general proved to be incompetent, the

Committee soon heard about it, and he was promptly replaced.

The very fact that the government was run by revolutionaries gave it a tremendous advantage in waging the war. In
all the other nations of Europe, the armies were commanded
by aristocrats, just as the former French army had been. Almost no one could become a general unless he belonged to a
noble family. Very often, indeed, the commanding generals
were given their jobs because they were close relatives of the
reigning king or emperor. Such generals might lose one battle after another but they were rarely dismissed, for few
rulers were prepared to dismiss their old friends, or their
brothers or cousins.

The Jacobins operated differently. They cared nothing
about a man's social position. All they cared about was that a
general should be a good soldier and loyal to the government.
Within a few months, the French army had a completely new
set of commanders. Most of them were young men, eager and
keen to fight. And because they had earned their positions by
their successes in battle, they were all brilliant commanders.

The French also had another tremendous advantage over
their enemies. They had a cause which they still believed in
with passion; the Revolution. One day, the famous woman
pianist Madame de Montgerout was arrested on suspicion of
treason. Because she had influential friends, she was brought
in front of the Committee of Public Safety to be questioned.
The Committee was doubtful about her, until one member
pointed to a piano and asked her to play the *"Marseillaise."*
As she played, the Committee members began to sing. Amazed
by the sound, clerks and secretaries rushed into the room,
and they, too, joined in the chorus. Soon, hundreds of voices
were echoing throughout the Tuileries Palace, all raised in

the marching battle song of the Revolution. Finally, everyone went back to work, and Madame de Montgerout was released. By playing the *"Marseillaise"* she had convinced the
Committee of her loyalty. And the sudden outbreak was
enormously revealing. For it showed how deep a faith lay
at the heart of the Revolution.

This faith was shared by the ordinary soldiers out on the
battlefields. They, too, felt they had something to fight for.
Before the French Revolution, military affairs had been quite
different. Most soldiers didn't care in the least about their
country or about their king. They fought only because they
were being paid or because they knew that if they threw
down their arms and ran, they would be shot.

But the soldiers of France did have a cause. They had the
Revolution. Everywhere in the army they heard talk about
liberty and equality. They listened to patriotic lectures given
by Jacobins sent out from Paris. Military bands inspired
them with the thundering chorus of the *"Marseillaise"* or
cheered them up with the gay, rollicking strains of the revolutionary dance, the *"Ça Ira."* The soldiers saw the tricolor,
the symbol of liberty, flapping in the wind over their barracks; they saw it again on the battlefield, raised high in the
midst of danger. They saw that if they fought well, peasants
or workingmen like themselves were promoted to be ser-
geants, and then lieutenants; and that lieutenants could be
promoted to be generals. Gradually, the ordinary French soldiers realized that they were being led not by the hated aristocrats, but by men of their own kind. In this atmosphere of
good fellowship, they came to feel that they were all serving
together in the cause of liberty and for the glory of France.

Inspired by the enthusiasm of their leaders, the French
army became the first truly national army in history. And to

their enthusiasm was added the fighting skill of their generals. The old-fashioned armies of Austria and Prussia could
not stand up against this combination. From the summer of
1793, the French armies began to win victories, and they kept
on winning them: over the Spaniards, the Austrians, and the
Prussians. Once again, they saved France from the invaders.
In fact, they did more. They advanced into Belgium, they in-
vaded Spain, they threatened Italy. So, while at home their
parents, their brothers, and their sisters suffered under the
Terror, the ardent young soldiers of the Revolution were
carrying the tricolor flag of liberty out across the border of
France and into the other countries of western Europe.

Eng.d by T.W. Hunt

DANTON

# CHAPTER ELEVEN

# THE TERROR

B Y THE end of the year 1793, Robespierre and his supporters had an iron grip over all France. In every city and village, the Jacobins were in control. Whatever they might do, no one dared to protest or to criticize. For, under the rule of the Jacobins, any word of criticism was considered treason. If anyone spoke against the government, the police were liable to come to his house in the middle of the night, arrest him and drag him away. If he was lucky, he would only be flung into jail. If he was unlucky, he would be brought up in front of the Revolutionary Tribunal and, almost certainly, be condemned to death.

Legally, it was the Convention, made up of the elected representatives of the people, who controlled the government. But it was the Committee of Public Safety which actually governed France. Robespierre was its most powerful member, and, by the winter of 1793, he had managed to make himself almost a dictator; a supremely powerful man who could do whatever he wished.

Now Robespierre was an extremely nervous man. He had for years lived in a state of perpetual fear, constantly suspicious that his enemies were plotting against him. It would seem logical that, as he became more powerful, he would have become less frightened. But exactly the opposite happened: Robespierre grew more frightened all the time. This often happens with dictators. Adolf Hitler, the Nazi dictator of Germany in the 1930's, lived in constant fear of plots against him. So did Josef Stalin, the Communist dictator of Russia for nearly thirty years. Both these men were so frightened that they set up an elaborate organization of secret police whose job was to listen for any mention of plots or conspiracies, or even any criticisms of the government. If they came to suspect anyone of plotting against them, Hitler or Stalin would instantly have him executed. Robespierre behaved in the same way. He, too, set up his own private network of secret police. And he, too, was ready to order the execution of anyone who might be dangerous to him.

But who did he have to fear? The aristocrats had all been killed or driven from France. The few nonjuring priests who still survived in Paris were all in hiding. There were, of course, tens of thousands of Frenchmen who had supported the Girondins, or who had been neutral in the struggle between them and the Jacobins. The great majority of these men were still at liberty. In fact, well over a hundred of them still sat as deputies in the Convention. But they were so scared of Robespierre that they would never have dared to conspire against him, and Robespierre knew it.

Of all the people in France, there was only one man Robespierre really had to fear. That man was his old rival, Georges Danton. Weary of the bloodshed, sickened by the never-ending talk of conspiracies and plots, Danton had practically retired from politics. Still, he remained a national hero. He was the man who had saved Paris in its most desperate hour, and few Frenchmen had forgotten that. He had supporters on all sides. The moderates, who loathed Robespierre, had come to like Danton. And he also had friends among the extreme Jacobins who now controlled France. For he had been one of their leaders since the start of the Revolution.

The news of the ghastly massacres at Toulon and Nantes and Lyons had filled Danton with horror. He hated the police spies who thronged the streets of Paris, and the loutish bullies in the local vigilance committees. He hated to see men and women who were no danger to the Revolution being dragged up in front of the Revolutionary Tribunal and condemned to die. Danton had always been brave and he dared to speak out. The victories of her armies, he declared, had made France safe. The Terror was completely unnecessary. It should be brought to an end, and the men and women of France should be allowed to enjoy in peace the benefits the Revolution had brought them.

Nothing could have angered or frightened Robespierre more. Somehow he had managed to convince himself that terror and fear were absolutely necessary for "the good of the people." It is hard to understand exactly what Robespierre meant when he talked about the good of the people, except that he wanted them all to be as prim and respectable as himself. But he certainly had come to believe that whatever he believed was right. Even when he changed his mind, he was still right; and if anyone else failed to change his mind at the same time, then that person was a traitor. That was the way Robespierre's mind worked. Anybody who disagreed with him was an enemy of France, a conspirator, plotting to betray the Revolution.

Thus, from Robespierre's point of view, Danton was now a traitor. For the good of France, he had to be executed. No doubt Robespierre also had other reasons for wanting to destroy Danton. He had always been envious of his rival's enormous vigor and strength; of his popularity and of the pleasure he managed to get out of life. What a triumph it would be then to Robespierre to crush this man and send him to the guillotine.

So the stage was set for the great battle between them. Who would win? Powerful as he was, Robespierre had to be very careful, and we must understand why. Legally, remember, the Convention was the ruling body of France. It had handed over the job of governing France to the Committee of Public Safety. For several months, the deputies in the Convention had agreed to every action the Committee recommended. Still, at any time the deputies could vote to replace the members of the Committee. Or, if they wished, they could abolish the Committee altogether.

There were two other complications. The Convention had also set up another committee, called the Committee of General Security. Its job was to run the police departments of France and it was very powerful. Robespierre could not afford to quarrel with it. Besides, the Committees themselves did not have the power to send "traitors" in front of the Revolutionary Tribunal. Only the Convention could do that. So, in order to destroy Danton, Robespierre had to perform two main tasks. He had first to persuade the members of the two committees to go along with his plan. Then he had to persuade a majority of the deputies in the Convention that Danton should be executed.

Knowing Robespierre as he did, Danton realized that his rival wanted to have him executed. However, he had always despised Robespierre and for a long time he refused to believe that he was in any danger. To a friend who warned him of what the Committee of Public Safety might do, Danton replied contemptuously, "They would not dare. Tell Robespierre that I will crush him in the palm of my hand when I think it necessary."

But Danton soon began to be less confident. When he spoke out against the Terror in the Convention, he found that most of the deputies, terrified of Robespierre, listened to him in icy silence. Weary and worried, Danton decided to make a personal appeal to Robespierre. He paid a visit to his old enemy and urged that they work together for the benefit of France. More than seventy deputies, he pointed out, were in prison. Perhaps they had been critical of the Terror. Still, they were good Jacobins, good revolutionaries, loyal to their country. He begged Robespierre to arrange for their release from jail.

"The only way to establish liberty," Robespierre replied coldly, "is to cut the heads off such criminals."

In his rage at this reply and perhaps also in despair, Danton burst into tears. Now, with his gift for spotting weakness in others, Robespierre realized that his opportunity to destroy Danton was approaching. He saw that Danton had grown weary; that he was no longer the forceful, inspiring leader he had been a year before. A few days later, the two men met again, this time by accident in a theater. A tragedy was being performed and, during the play, an actor spoke the words: "Down with the tyrant." A group of friends who were sitting near Danton looked up at Robespierre who was in a box above them, and shook their fists at him. Robespierre responded with a curious movement of his hand; waving it, said an observer, "in a gesture that expressed both fear and menace."

Fear and menace. It was clear now to Danton's friends

that the decisive moment was fast approaching, and they urged Danton to prepare. He must rally his supporters, they insisted, and prepare to fight. Or, if he would not do that, he must flee from France to safety. But Danton would not flee and he would not fight either.

"It would only mean the shedding of more blood," he said slowly. "There has been enough. It is better to be guillotined than to guillotine."

Obviously some kind of fatal weakness had come over Danton. He was like a man who, carried out to sea on an outgoing tide, has struggled until his strength is gone, and then, exhausted, allows himself to be sucked under the waves. While Danton waited, Robespierre set about preparing the decisive blow. Night after night he sat up alone writing out in detail his reasons for believing that Danton was a traitor. Towards the end of March, he handed over his notes to his faithful ally St. Just, and instructed him to draw up a formal accusation against Danton.

The next task was to persuade the other members of the Committee of Public Safety to agree to Danton's arrest. It was not easy. When St. Just produced his list of charges, a violent quarrel broke out around the oval table. Lindet, the Quartermaster-General, refused to sign his name to the charges. "I am here to feed citizens," he declared, "not to put patriots to death." Another old friend of Danton's also refused to sign his name. But the other members of the Committee supported Robespierre. For they believed what St. Just told them: "If we do not guillotine him, we shall be guillotined ourselves."

Once it had reached its decision the Committee acted with its usual speed. That same night Danton and a dozen of his friends were arrested. One of them, Hérault de Séchelles, was still officially a member of the Committee of Public Safety. Another, Camille Desmoulins, was the journalist who, four years earlier, had jumped up onto a table and rallied the crowd to storm the Bastille. Desmoulins had been at school with Robespierre and for years had been his closest friend. Robespierre had been the best man at his wedding and was the godfather of his young son. But none of that stopped him. Desmoulins had criticized him in the newspapers and that was something Robespierre could not forgive. If Desmoulins had criticized him, then Desmoulins was a traitor and, old friend or not, he had to die.

The news that Danton and his friends had actually been arrested came as a tremendous shock. Even the most ardent Jacobins were stunned. Inside the Convention the news was received with absolute horror. It was filled with deputies who had been Danton's allies only two years before when the revolutionaries were struggling to seize power from the King and the aristocrats. These men might not have been ready to support Danton in criticizing the Terror, but they simply could not believe that he was guilty of treason. One of them was Legendre, the former butcher who had led a Paris mob into the Tuileries Palace and there had delivered a savage speech against the King. Determined to save his old friend, Legendre made an impassioned speech.

"I am convinced," he shouted, "that Danton is as innocent as myself."

A murmur of approval came from the benches around the Convention chamber. Made bold by Legendre's lead, other deputies arose and declared that Danton must be allowed to come before the Convention to answer the charges made against him. He was, they said, a member of the Convention. As such, he should not be sent to trial without first being heard.

While one of these deputies was pleading for Danton, Robespierre entered the chamber. The moment was decisive. The Convention was on the verge of revolt. If a majority of the deputies supported Danton, they might destroy the Committee of Public Safety. Then it might well be Robespierre and St. Just who would go to the guillotine instead of Danton.

At this vital moment, Robespierre made supreme use of his mysterious power to terrorize his opponents. When Legendre demanded an explanation of Danton's arrest, Robespierre went to the rostrum. After delivering a violent attack against Danton, he went on: "We shall see this day whether the Convention will be able to destroy a pretended idol long since rotted away; or whether in its fall it will crush the Convention and the people of France."

The deputies had long since fallen silent. In the tense stillness, Robespierre paused. He turned his cold stare on Legendre, and the normally self confident ex-butcher positively trembled in his seat with fear. "The man who trembles at my glance," Robespierre went on, "is himself guilty."

Thoroughly cowed, Legendre rose and stammered out an apology for trying to defend Danton. Robespierre had never been so terrifying. The entire Convention was entirely in his grip and the revolt was completely crushed. Leaving the rostrum, Robespierre made way for St. Just to read out the formal charges against Danton. He, too, was a terrifying figure. Years afterwards, a deputy who was there that day still remembered how the hand of the Archangel of Death rose and fell, rose and fell, as he spoke, like the falling blade of the guillotine.

Without any further protest, the deputies voted to send Danton before the Revolutionary Tribunal. They also set about making absolutely sure that he would be found guilty. Special jurors were picked for the trial; all of them personal enemies of Danton. And both the jurors and the judges were given a deadly warning. If Danton was not found guilty, they themselves might be executed.

Danton's position seemed to be hopeless. But now, with his death so close, all his old courage and vigor seemed to flood back into him. He was determined to go down fighting. Brought before the Tribunal, he spoke out in the voice that once had rallied France. It rang through the courtroom and out over the streets outside. There people gathered by the hundreds to listen spellbound as Danton denounced his enemies on the Committee of Public Safety, and tore to shreds the charges against him.

One of the charges was that he had supported the monarchy and tried to save Louis the Sixteenth and Marie Antoinette.

"Danton an aristocrat," he bellowed. "France will not believe that story long. The people will tear my enemies in pieces before three months are out. My name is associated with every revolutionary institution; the revolutionary army, the revolutionary committees, the Committee of Public Safety, the Revolutionary Tribunal. Why, I have brought about my own death."

Every word he spoke was true and, listening, his audience remembered. Indeed it was Danton himself who had set up the Committee of Public Safety. It was Danton who had organized the first revolutionary armies. It was Danton who had suggested the creation of the Revolutionary Tribunal, the very Tribunal that was now about to condemn him to

G

death. The idea that this man could be a traitor to the Revolution was absurd. Soon, every sentence was bringing
murmurs of approval from the crowds who thronged the
streets and from the spectators in the galleries around the
courtroom.

There was no stopping Danton. He had talked for more
than an hour and it was clear that the charges brought
against him could not possibly be true. Moment by moment
Fouquier-Tinville and the judges became more alarmed.
Somehow Danton had to be silenced before the crowds
started to demand that he and his friends be set free. The
judges therefore sent a message to the Committee of Public
Safety asking for help, and the Committee immediately responded.

Danton, it decided, was attacking the Revolutionary Tribunal. And the Revolutionary Tribunal was a part of the
government. That meant Danton was guilty of plotting
against the government. A new law was needed. Anyone who
attacked the "national justice" could be silenced whenever
the judges of the Tribunal wished it.

Blindly obedient, like sheep, the deputies of the Convention passed the new law, and one of them rushed to the Tribunal, carrying the decree in his hand.

"This should help you," he said, handing it to Fouquier-
Tinville.

"Indeed, we need it," replied the Prosecutor, smiling, and
he read out the decree. Danton could speak no longer. He was
not allowed to question the witnesses against him. Such a
law, of course, made the whole idea of the "trial" ridiculous.
Three deputies from the Convention were standing at one
side of the courtroom, and Danton turned on them savagely.
"You are murderers," he bellowed at them. "Murderers.

Look at them," he appealed to the spectators in the galleries. "They have hounded us to our deaths." Then he picked out the man whose hand lay behind the whole plot against him. "Vile Robespierre," he shouted. "You, too, will go to the scaffold. You will follow me, Robespierre."

His words electrified the spectators, and shouts and protests rang out all around the courtroom. Trying to restore order, the presiding judge rang his bell and declared that "the debate will now end."

"End!" yelled Danton in a fury. "How can it end? It hasn't even begun. You have not called a single witness. You have not read a single document. We are to be sentenced without a hearing."

But his protests were futile. The Convention had acted and the Convention could make whatever laws it pleased. The trial was over. Yet the judges were still so afraid of Danton that they did not even allow him to be brought back into the courtroom to hear the sentence. They were determined to keep him out of sight so that he could not arouse the people any further. He and his friends were therefore left inside their cells when the jury returned to the courtroom, and the foreman announced with glee: "The wretches are going to die."

The Revolution's "justice" was swift. Men who were condemned one day went to the guillotine on the next. On the afternoon after the trial, Danton and the other convicted men were taken from the Conciergerie prison and led into the carts that were to take them to their death. The horse-drawn carts, bearing their cargo of doomed men and women, had long since become a familiar sight in Paris, and few people now turned out to watch them go by. But this procession was different. Danton, the hero of the Revolution, was going to his death, and hundreds of thousands of Parisians assembled to watch him ride by. Few of them could have felt much joy as they looked at his huge figure, towering over his companions, and at his ugly, familiar face as he stared around him in proud contempt. For surely the thought must have occurred to most of the spectators: "If this man, once our idol, can be sent to the guillotine, who among us can feel safe?"

Camille Desmoulins, who had always been a weakling, could not believe that the people would let him die. His face streaming with tears, he cried out to the watching crowds: "People, they have lied to you. They are sacrificing your servants."

Danton made no such appeals. These were the men and women for whom he had fought. These were the ordinary people he had loved and had saved from the vengeance of the émigré nobles. But, from fear of Robespierre, not one would lift a hand to save him, and he despised them for their cowardice.

"Be quiet," he said to Desmoulins. "Leave that vile rabble alone."

As they approached the square where the guillotine towered against the sky, the carts passed the house where Robespierre lived. But, on this day of his greatest victory, Robespierre chose to keep out of sight, and the shutters were drawn tight across the windows of his home. For a moment, as the carts rumbled past, Danton lost his self-control. "Vile Robespierre," he shouted up at the closed shutters, just as he had shouted in the courtroom. "You will follow me."

After that he was silent. It was late afternoon by the time the carts reached the guillotine, and Sanson, the executioner, was in a hurry to get the business finished before darkness fell. As the victims stood on the platform, waiting their turn to be thrust under the knife, Hérault de Séchelles turned to embrace Danton and bid him a last farewell. Sanson thrust them apart. "Fool," exclaimed Danton contemptuously. "You will not be able to keep our heads from kissing in the basket."

The knife fell. De Séchelles was dead. Now it was Danton's turn. For a moment, as he thought of the young wife he loved, he was overcome by weakness. "Oh, my beloved," he murmured, "shall I never see you again?" Then he pulled himself together, and is was with his old defiance that he faced his death.

"Don't forget to show my head to the people," he said to the executioner. "It is worth the trouble."

Then he, too, was dead. The Revolution had murdered its greatest hero.

The execution of Danton naturally made Robespierre more powerful than ever. Two of the other members of the Committee of Public Safety, St. Just and Couthon, were completely loyal to him. The rest were ready to let him have his way. Now, for several horrible weeks, the Terror reached its peak.

Many people who lived through those weeks have described the atmosphere of fear that hung over Paris. The citizens lived in a state of constant dread. It was as if some horrible plague had attacked the city and no one knew who might catch it next. Theaters closed, and restaurants, cabarets, and other places of entertainment. If they had stayed open, they would have been empty. Few Parisians were ready to venture out after dark, because anyone seen in the streets at night was liable to be seized by the roving bands of security guards. The citizens preferred to stay home with the doors of their houses locked and the shutters bolted over the windows. But even behind the locked doors, there was no safety against the police. A harsh knock might sound at any time of the day or night. Outside a group of security police would be standing. "Citizen, you have been reported to be plotting against the Revolution." That was all that needed to be said, and the unfortunate victim would be hustled away.

Every week the numbers of arrests mounted until there was scarcely enough room in the prisons to hold the accused "conspirators." Most often the prisoners did not even know why they had been arrested. There were no charges for them to answer. They had simply been denounced by some unknown police spy or informer. Or the local vigilance committee had ordered them to be arrested. And if they were lucky enough not to be sent to the guillotine, they were left to rot in prison.

This was the time when any malicious Frenchman could take his revenge on an old enemy by denouncing him as a traitor. In this atmosphere, ordinary men and women could no longer speak freely. Almost every subject was dangerous. If a man spoke of some happy time a few years before, he was likely to be accused of being a supporter of the old regime. Therefore he was an enemy of the Revolution. If he complained about the shortage of food, or about the war, he was also an enemy of the Revolution. No one could be trusted. An old friend might turn out to be a secret police spy. It was dangerous even to look unhappy.

The Terror was not aimed only at the rich. Indeed by the spring of 1794, most of those arrested were ordinary working men or women. The most ridiculous accusations could be fatal. One poor woman happened to remark that she wanted a spinning wheel. And because the French word for spinning wheel (*rouet*) sounded like the word for king (*roi*), she was accused of being a "royalist" and guillotined. Often mistakes were made, names were confused in the police files, and the wrong man or woman was arrested. But because he did not know why he had been arrested, the victim did not know a mistake had been made and he would go, in bewilderment, to the guillotine.

As the Terror mounted, so did the number of trials in front of the Revolutionary Tribunal. With so many accused to be dealt with, there was no time to listen to the evidence. It was useless to plead innocence. The mere fact that anyone had been accused was enough for the Tribunal to find him guilty. Fouquier-Tinville had been given his job: to obtain verdicts of guilty; and he pursued it relentlessly.

"You do not deny the charge against you, citizen?" he would ask.

"I do not understand. I have done nothing."

"You will understand soon enough." And Fouquier-Tinville would turn to the jurors. "Is it not enough, members of the jury, that this wretch confesses to doing nothing while the fate of France is at stake? You must find him guilty."

"Guilty," would be the verdict.

And the sentence, from the judges: "To the guillotine."

Shopkeepers, workmen, an occasional priest, old men in their eighties, girls too young to know what the Revolution was all about: separately or in batches they were brought before the Tribunal and condemned to death. In front of it there appeared also some of the generals who had commanded the first revolutionary armies. One was Biron, the General whose orders had been voted on by his men. Another was General Houchard, a giant of a man with his mouth twisted by gunshot wounds, his upper lip split in two by a saber cut, and two parallel gashes in his right cheek.

"Why did you not capture the whole of the Austrian army?" he was asked.

Houchard gave a growl of disgust. The President of the Tribunal called him a coward and Houchard, in his rage, jumped up and tore open his shirt, revealing a chest scarred with bullet wounds.

"Citizen jurymen," he exclaimed. "Read my reply. It is written here." Then, falling back into his seat, he burst into tears of fury, repeating, "He called me a coward. He called me a coward." And though Houchard had risked his life over and over again, fighting for the Revolution, he, too, was sent to the guillotine.

General Kellermann, who had helped win the vital battle of Valmy, was another victim. So was Lavoisier, perhaps the most brilliant chemist of the century. So was André de Chénier, one of France's greatest poets, executed by error because he was mistaken for his brother.

Still, occasionally the judges and jurors of the Revolutionary Tribunal did bring in a verdict of innocent. This infuriated Robespierre and he arranged for a new president of the Tribunal to be appointed. This man, Dumas, was a close friend of Robespierre's, and he was so brutal that even Fouquier-Tinville described him as a "strangler." Dumas positively gloated with pleasure as he pronounced the sentences of death, and his job was made easier by yet another law which Robespierre insisted on having passed. This law, called the Law of 22 Prairial, stated that there was no need for detailed accusations to be made. In other words, Fouquier-Tinville did not even need to pretend that he had evidence against the men and women dragged before the Tribunal. All he had to do was to assert that the accused had 'conspired against the people." Nor could the accused speak in their own defense. If Dumas was satisfied with the "evidence," then the jury could bring in its verdict. Naturally it was always guilty.

This was the way Danton had been condemned. The whole idea of justice was now a complete farce. Every day the so-called "enemies of the people" waited in their prisons for the dreaded roll call. If their name was on it, they had to go before the Tribunal and that, as they all knew, meant death.

And every day the number of names on the roll call grew larger. Forty names a day, fifty, sixty . . .

"Heads," wrote Fouquier-Tinville in delight, "are falling like slates. Next week I'll take the tops off three or four hundred." By this time, the sight of the carts rumbling through the streets had become part of the everyday life of Paris. There were some people, probably half crazy, who still went every day to watch the sight of heads dropping into the basket. But most Parisians had grown to hate the death carts, rumbling by with their daily load of victims. They tried to keep away from the streets traveled by the tumbrils. The sight of innocent people being carried to the guillotine reminded them that they themselves might be the next to die.

With so many executions taking place, the paving stones around the guillotine became so drenched with blood that a horrible smell arose from them. As it happened, many important officials lived near the square where the guillotine stood. One of them was Robespierre. Although he and his friends were responsible for the executions, most of them disliked the smell of blood. So the guillotine was moved to another square, in a district inhabited by poor working men and women, far from the center of the city. There, no one of im-

H

portance had to suffer from the smell. And as the carts no longer passed through the center of Paris, most of its citizens could pretend they did not know just how many people were being murdered.

As the months passed, the atmosphere of fear hung more and more heavily over Paris and the other large cities of France. By the early summer of 1794 it looked as if there were no way to drive Robespierre and his followers from power; or to bring the Terror to an end. The guillotine, with its blade ever falling, falling, falling, seemed to have become a permanent part of the life of France.

Raffet del.                                    Lecouturier sc.

TALLIEN

# CHAPTER TWELVE

# THE END OF THE REVOLUTION

I N THE SUMMER of 1794 there must have been hundreds of thousands of Frenchmen who would willingly have returned to the old conditions before the Revolution. And the politicians in Paris would perhaps have been among the most eager to turn the clock back. They, of all people, were in the worst danger. At any moment the eye of Robespierre might fall on them; suspicious, calculating, menacing. How could they ever be free of him? There was only one answer. If the members of the Committee of Public Safety began to fall out among themselves, then the power of Robespierre might be broken at last.

Actually that moment was quickly approaching. For nearly a year the members of the Committee had sat around the same table. From early in the morning until far into the night, they had been working without a break. All the time they had labored under the terrible strain of trying to bring order to France. Under the strain, the nerves of many had reached the breaking point and some had grown to hate others with a bitter loathing.

Much of this loathing was personal. Carnot, who was in charge of the army, detested St. Just, who was continually interfering with his plans. St. Just, in return, hated Carnot. Lindet, the Quartermaster-General, had not forgiven Robespierre and St. Just for sending Danton to the guillotine. But much of the bitterness that seethed around the oval table arose out of fear. Often the most brutal men are the most fearful and this was certainly the case among the members of the Committee of Public Safety. Two of them, Collot d'Herbois and Billaud-Varenne, had been among the most savage of the terrorists. As much as anyone, they had been responsible for the butchery of the Terror. Yet, as the Terror reached its height, these two men became increasingly afraid. They were afraid of Robespierre. And they feared him because they knew he looked down on them as bloodthirsty assassins who were interested only in seizing more power for themselves. It might seem surprising that Robespierre, of all people, should despise other people for being bloodthirsty. But Robespierre always thought of himself as a man who had the good of the people at heart. He had honestly managed to convince himself that he only ordered executions in order to preserve the revolutionary principles of liberty and equality. He despised Collot d'Herbois and Billaud-Varenne for not caring about the Revolution.

Both his enemies knew full well how skillfully Robespierre could intrigue to get rid of people he hated. They remembered the fate that had befallen the Girondin leaders; and Danton; and Camille Desmoulins, who had once been Robespierre's closest friend. They had no doubt that, when it suited him, Robespierre would not hesitate to send them also to the guillotine.

At the end of June, a violent quarrel broke out inside the Committee which ended with Robespierre storming out of the room with tears of frustrated anger pouring down his face. We do not know what had upset him. Perhaps he had demanded the execution of yet another batch of deputies from the Convention and had been refused. Probably his closest allies, St. Just and Couthon, had voted with him. But Collot d'Herbois and Billaud-Varenne would probably have voted against him. And they may have been supported by Carnot, Lindet, and other members of the Committee.

For several weeks after that meeting, Robespierre stayed away from the Committee. He rarely stirred out of his home. His excuse was that he was sick, and probably it was true. A man can become sick from nervous fear and Robespierre, as he became more powerful, had become ever more nervous. Everywhere he imagined plots and intrigues against him. Sometime during those weeks, he must finally have decided to destroy his enemies, and, while he remained in his home, he prepared his plans : to send them to the guillotine.

Few people could have known exactly what Robespierre was planning. But during the last weeks of June and the early weeks of July, a growing fear of what he would do next spread among the politicians in Paris. This fear was especially strong among the deputies in the Convention. For only the Convention could send suspected enemies of the people in front of the Revolutionary Tribunal. To get rid of his rivals, Robespierre absolutely had to keep control of the Convention. And the obvious way for him to do that was to get rid of any deputies who might oppose him.

Who would he strike against? The deputies waited and trembled. Many tried to avoid danger by keeping out of the way. Already hundreds of seats in the chamber were empty. They were the ones that had once been occupied by the Girondins, or by Danton and his friends. Now other gaps appeared among the benches. Dozens of deputies arranged to be away from Paris, while many who remained never slept two nights running in the same house, in case Robespierre's police might suddenly appear and arrest them.

It was inevitable that sooner or later, these terrified men should reach the obvious conclusion. Was it really necessary to be so afraid of Robespierre? Suppose all those who feared him agreed to stick together? Suppose they could outvote the deputies who remained loyal to Robespierre? Then he would be helpless.

So, while Robespierre was preparing his trap, his enemies set about preparing a trap of their own. Because their plans were so secret, we do not know exactly who was involved. Certainly Collot d'Herbois and Billaud-Varenne were among the plotters. Probably Carnot and Lindet and other members of the Committee of Public Safety joined with them. So did many deputies who were not members of the Committee.

It was a neck-and-neck race and it was Robespierre who struck first. For weeks, while secluded in his home, he had worked on a speech in which he planned to denounce his enemies as "conspirators" against the Revolution. On the afternoon of July 26, he came to the rostrum in the Convention chamber to deliver it. Haggard and fearful, the deputies gazed at the papers Robespierre was clutching. Somewhere among those papers, as they all knew, there was a list of names of the men he wanted executed. And every one of the deputies was wondering: Is my name on it?

Robespierre had been up all the previous night, putting the final touches on his speech. His face was white and drawn from lack of sleep and from the strain of the last few weeks. But the power he had wielded for so long had made him more arrogant than ever, and his speech was full of menace.

The financial system of the country, he told the deputies, had been mismanaged. That remark was a threat against Cambon, the Minister of Finance. The war was not being managed properly. That was a threat against Carnot. Then, with truly astonishing boldness, Robespierre went on to hint that the Terror, the Terror he himself had organized, had really been a plot against the people of France.

"The conspirators," he declared, "have accomplices in the General Security Committee. Certain members of the Committee of Public Safety are also guilty." And what was to be done? Robespierre had his answer ready. The Committee of General Security had to be reorganized. The Committee of Public Safety had to be "purified."

The deputies listened with stupefied horror. This was worse than anything they had anticipated. Robespierre was not just condemning a few individuals. He was criticizing everything the government had done for the past year. He was attacking his most loyal supporters: the extreme revolutionaries who had controlled the government and organized the Terror. That meant that almost anyone's name might be on the list which was surely among the papers he was holding.

Robespierre had grown so used to getting his own way that he must have expected his speech to go unchallenged. He had set the stage and the next day St. Just would come before the Convention to demand the arrest of the deputies who were to be sent before the Revolutionary Tribunal. That was how Robespierre had arranged his intrigue against Danton. But this time, there were deputies ready to fight back, and one of them was Cambon, the Minister of Finance.

Almost as soon as Robespierre had finished speaking, Cambon hurried to the rostrum. "Before I am dishonored," he cried, "I will speak to France. It is time that everyone

H*

here should know the truth. One man paralyzes the will of the National Convention. That man is Robespierre."

Encouraged by Cambon's boldness, other deputies followed his lead. "Robespierre has drawn up a list," one of them began, "and my name is said to be on it . . ."

He was interrupted by a storm of other deputies. "The list!" they shouted. "The list!"

"Name those whom you have accused."

"Name them. Name them."

But Robespierre would not mention any more names. He was determined to stick to his original plan. He had thrown out his hints and, by arousing the fear of the deputies, he had prepared them to condemn the people St. Just would name on the following day. Still Robespierre was disturbed by the opposition to him in the Convention, and that night he turned for support to the men who had launched him on his way to power. He appeared in front of the Jacobin Club. In that dark and gloomy chamber, lit by the flickering light of candles, he repeated his speech to the sansculottes who were gathered there. These were the toughs, the mobsters who had always idolized Robespierre the Incorruptible, the enemy of the aristocrats. These were the ignorant bullies who made up the local vigilance committees and reveled in their authority over the respectable men and women who had always been their superiors. It was Robespierre who had given them their authority and they trusted him absolutely. When he spoke of "conspirators" high in the government, they filled the chamber with boos and hisses. When he told them that the conspirators must be destroyed, they banged their glasses on the rough tables and roared that the enemies of the people must go to the guillotine.

Collot d'Herbois and Billaud-Varenne had been among

the first members of the Jacobin Club and that night they went there to see what was happening. To their horror, they found that their old comrades had turned against them. Knowing they were among the "conspirators" Robespierre had denounced, the sansculottes greeted them with a storm of threats. Dumas, the president of the Revolutionary Tribunal, was presiding over the meeting, and he turned to Collot d'Herbois and Billaud-Varenne with a leer of triumph.

"I look forward to seeing you two in the Tribunal tomorrow," he said.

The two men hesitated and suddenly a mob of sansculottes rushed toward them. "Kill them," they shouted. "To the guillotine with them." Collot was closer to the door and he managed to escape before the mob could reach him. But Billaud-Varenne was caught, thrown to the floor, and beaten before he managed to break away.

Robespierre had proved that the sansculottes of Paris were still firmly behind him. When the Convention met at noon on the following day, the deputies saw it also. From front to back, the public galleries were packed with sansculottes. Just before noon, Robespierre entered the chamber. He was dressed with his usual care, in a pale blue coat and yellow breeches, and his hair was carefully powdered. He looked exactly like the aristocrats he was always attacking; but as he came in, the mob in the galleries set up a roar of cheers. Hearing them, Robespierre seemed to walk on air. Obviously brimming with confidence, he took a seat directly in front of the rostrum where St. Just was due to stand while he delivered his speech.

But it was not the spectators who would decide the future of France on that fateful day. It was the deputies who would do the voting. Few of them had slept the night before. They had all been too nervous and busy to go to bed. All night they had been talking, intriguing and calculating, trying to decide which side was the stronger. About the people they cared nothing. Their only concern was to preserve their own lives by voting with the winning side.

Still, it would be unfair to blame them too harshly. Looking to one side of the chamber, the deputies could see the empty seats that had once been occupied by the leaders of the Girondins. On the opposite side, they could see the empty seats where Danton and his friends had sat. Now the final showdown was coming, and the price of the wrong choice would be death. It is surely no wonder that on that morning an atmosphere of dread and of feverish excitement filled the chamber. For no one could tell which side would win. In fact the uncertainty was so great that one member of the Committee of Public Safety, Barère, is said to have come to the chamber with two speeches in his pocket: one supporting Robespierre and one condemning him.

For a year the extreme Jacobins had dominated the Convention. But now they were split; some siding with Robespierre, others with Collot d'Herbois, Billaud-Varenne, and the other conspirators. About sixty of the deputies who were loyal to Robespierre were away from Paris on missions for the government. Thus, the decision would rest with the moderate deputies; the men who had once supported the Girondins or had been neutral between them and the Jacobins. They were terrified of Robespierre. On the other hand, they would surely seize their chance to get rid of him so that they could live without fear.

Which way would they vote? Obviously the first indication would be the effect of St. Just's speech. If the deputies listened to him in awed silence, as they always had before, then

Robespierre would win. St. Just himself had no doubts. Like Robespierre, he was curiously foppish for a revolutionary and that morning he wore a chamois-colored coat, a white waistcoat, and pale gray breeches. His manner, as usual, was cold, haughty and arrogant as, looking neither to right nor left, he strode to the rostrum and prepared to speak.

It did not seem to occur either to Robespierre or to St. Just that anyone would dare to challenge them. Despite the protests made against Robespierre on the previous day, both he and his faithful ally were completely self-assured. Perhaps they were so sure they were doing the right thing that they assumed a majority of the deputies would agree with them. Or perhaps they had grown to despise the deputies who had always obeyed their slightest wishes. Such weaklings, they might have felt, would never dare to stand up against them. In any case, they were very soon to discover how wrong they were. For St. Just had only spoken two sentences when he was interrupted by a deputy named Tallien, who knew that his name was on Robespierre's list of the men who were to die.

"I demand to be heard," Tallien called out.

St. Just was taken by surprise and he protested indignantly. Such a thing had never happened before. It was impossible that he should be interrupted. That day, however, the president of the Convention was Collot d'Herbois who knew, of course, that his name was also on the list. As president of the Convention, he had the right to decide who should speak. When St. Just tried to go on, Collot rang his bell to drown out his words.

Now, at last, the Archangel of Death seemed to understand what was happening. The men he was about to have executed had organized their plot. He and Robespierre had been outmaneuvered. Was it possible? He paused, shaken. For once his nerve seemed to fail and Tallien, rushing to the rostrum, pushed him to one side.

"I demand that the curtain be torn away," he cried. And from the floor of the Convention, Robespierre's enemies shouted out: "It must be."

Billaud-Varenne stepped forward to take Tallien's place, and he described what had happened the night before at the Jacobin Club.

"These people are planning to murder the Convention," he shouted.

Most of the moderate deputies had not known anything about that meeting. But they realized instantly the significance of what Billaud-Varenne had told them. Once before, the Paris mob had forced the Convention to bow to its wishes. Now Robespierre was appealing to the mob again. For a year, the Paris mob had been quiet, but if it was turned loose again in the streets, no one knew what might happen. What did Robespierre have in mind? Could he really be planning to use the mob to force the Convention to obey him? While they were wondering, Tallien returned to the rostrum. He, too, had been at the Jacobin Club on the previous night. There, he told the deputies, he had seen how a dictator was planning to form his own army to take over the government.

"I have armed myself," he declared, "with a dagger which shall pierce this man's breast if the Convention does not have the courage to decree his arrest." And, pulling a dagger out of his clothes, Tallien waved it threateningly in the air.

Actually Tallien was a brutal and cowardly terrorist who would never have had the courage to plunge a dagger into anyone, and certainly not into a man like Robespierre. But the sight of the dagger electrified the deputies, and, from the back of the chamber, one of them shouted out: "Down with the tyrant."

Though no one had yet dared to mention him by name, everyone knew who the tyrant was. As he heard the word, Robespierre, his face livid, sprang from his seat and dashed toward the rostrum. But his enemies were determined not to let him speak. They had seen only too often how he could reduce the Convention to terror and frighten the deputies into obeying him. With a few menacing words and glances, he had cowed them into voting for the execution of Danton. At all costs he had to be prevented from speaking. With his bell, Collot drowned out the sound of Robespierre's words from the floor of the chamber, while first one and then another of the conspirators stepped up to the rostrum, all resolved to keep Robespierre away.

Minute by minute, the conspirators were growing more confident. They had stood up to Robespierre. They had kept him silent, and they could see that the undecided deputies were turning against him. Now it was time to strike the next blow. Returning to the rostrum, Tallien asked the Convention to order the arrest of Robespierre's friend and ally, General Hanriot, commander of the Paris National Guard.

"Down with the tyrant," roared the deputies, and they voted to have Hanriot arrested.

Now Tallien asked for the arrest of another of Robespierre's closest friends, the brutal Dumas, president of the Revolutionary Tribunal.

Again the roar of "down with the tyrant" echoed through the chamber and the arrest of Dumas was ordered.

Hanriot and Dumas! They were two of the main props of Robespierre's power. One controlled with his soldiers the streets of Paris. The other made sure that the victims sent before his Tribunal went to the guillotine. Now they were lost, for their arrest would certainly mean their death. One by one, as if shearing away the claws of a great cat, the deputies were destroying Robespierre's ability to terrify them. The moment had come to strike at him directly and, at last, speaking from the back of the chamber, a deputy dared mention the name of the tyrant.

"I demand the arrest of Robespierre," he cried.

The Convention was practically in a state of chaos. In their excitement, the deputies had leaped to their feet, and the sound of their shouts and cheers drowned out the sound of the president's bell as he rang for order. Yet, with a desperate effort, Robespierre finally managed to make his voice heard. Above the uproar, the deputies could hear his words, shouted at Collot d'Herbois, in the president's chair: "For the last time, will you give me leave to speak, president of assassins?"

Probably Robespierre was already doomed. If he had not been, those words, torn from his throat, would have sealed his fate. "President of assassins!" He was calling the deputies "assassins." Who among them could doubt any longer that, if he was allowed to reassert his power, he might have all of them sent to the guillotine?

With perfect timing, Collot d'Herbois seized on that moment to ask the deputies to vote for Robespierre's arrest. Then, suddenly, Robespierre cracked. As St. Just had done a few minutes earlier, he too seemed to lose his nerve. In despair, he rushed toward the benches where he usually sat, among the extreme Jacobins, holding out his hands toward them, as if begging for help.

But those men, his former friends, would have none of him.

"Get away from here," one of them shouted. "The ghosts of Danton and Camille Desmoulins reject you."

Again Robespierre tried to speak but his voice was drowned in the shouting. "The blood of Danton is choking you," yelled another deputy.

Growing more desperate every moment, Robespierre turned to the moderates who sat in the center of the chamber. They, too, waved him back. Turning again, like a cornered animal, Robespierre scrambled up among the benches which had once been occupied by the Girondins, and collapsed panting on an empty seat. Nearby were the Girondins who had managed to escape the guillotine. For nearly a year they had obeyed Robespierre in order to save their own necks. But now they drew away from him in pretended horror.

"Monster," one shouted. "You are sitting where Vergniaud once sat."

Robespierre had only one place left to turn; to the Jacobins in the galleries, to the sansculottes who had for so long trusted and adored him. But those same Jacobins who had cheered him with rapture only a few minutes earlier now realized that he was doomed. They, too, were concerned only to save themselves. The ones who were known to be close supporters of Robespierre had already crept away from the chamber to safety. Those who still remained echoed the shouts of the deputies below.

"Arrest him," they kept on calling. "Arrest the monster."

The battle in the Convention was over. The conspirators had won. Quickly the deputies voted to arrest Robespierre and his friends, St. Just and Couthon. The three men were taken down to the floor in front of the president's chair, and while Collot d'Herbois looked down at them in triumph, the decree of arrest was read out. Then, under heavy guard, they were led away.

Overwhelmed with relief at their victory, the deputies let their feelings run free. They cheered, they laughed, they clapped each other on the shoulder, and embraced. They threw their hats in the air. They had won, they were safe. The monster was destroyed. No longer would any deputy have to tremble with fear when his menacing glare played over the chamber. Like so many of his own victims, Robespierre would very soon be sent in front of the Revolutionary Tribunal to be tried for conspiring against the people. He would be found guilty and within a day at most, his head, too, would fall into the basket.

So the deputies thought. But they were congratulating themselves too quickly. For although Robespierre had been defeated in the Convention, he still had powerful friends who might be able to save him. The toughs of the Paris streets were still on his side and so was the Commune, the city government of Paris. Just over a year earlier, the Commune and the mob, with the support of Hanriot's National Guardsmen had imposed their will on the Convention. They had forced the deputies to expel the Girondin leaders. Perhaps they could force the Convention to give way again.

The attempt to rally the Parisians against the Convention was led by one of Robespierre's closest allies: Fleuriot, the Mayor of Paris. While the triumphant deputies went off to celebrate their victory with a luxurious dinner, Fleuriot acted. To the Jacobin Club, which was packed with supporters of Robespierre, he sent a request that as many men (and women) as possible should gather in front of the City Hall. He also ordered the tocsin to be rung. As they heard the old familiar call to arms, other sansculottes began to pour·

out into the streets and make their way to the City Hall. Meanwhile Fleuriot gave orders that no prisoners should be admitted to the prisons that day. So, when Robespierre was brought under guard to the Luxembourg prison, the authorities refused to take him in, and instead of being shut up in a prison cell where he would have been helpless, Robespierre was allowed to stay free.

At this decisive moment, the fate of the Convention — and of France — depended mainly on General Hanriot, the commander of the National Guard. If he rallied his men, he could easily take over control of Paris and arrest the deputies who had voted against Robespierre. But Hanriot was a heavy drinker and, as it happened, he had been drunk throughout the whole fateful day. During the afternoon, he seemed to lose all control over himself. When he heard that the Convention had voted to arrest him, he jumped on his horse and started to gallop through the streets, waving his sword in the air and shouting: "Kill all policemen. Kill all policemen."

He kept on galloping until he was pulled off his horse by gendarmes who had been sent by the Convention. They took him away and shut him up in the offices of the Committee of Public Safety. But Hanriot was not there long, for the Commune quickly summoned two hundred soldiers and sent them to the Tuileries Palace to rescue their commander.

Now a desperate race began. By this time the deputies had realized the danger, and they set about collecting soldiers from all sections of Paris. Meanwhile the Commune, led by Fleuriot, was doing the same. At first it looked as if the Commune would win. By the hundreds, the sansculottes made their way to the City Hall to fight for their idol, Robespierre. If Robespierre could have summoned up the courage to put himself at the head of this makeshift army, he might still have been able to destroy his enemies. But Robespierre had never been a man of action. He was a speaker, a politician, an intriguer. Despite Fleuriot's continual appeals, he could not bring himself to go to the City Hall. He hesitated, he wavered. Not until eleven o'clock that night did he do as Fleuriot wished, and go to the City Hall to rally his supporters.

And by then it was too late. For while the evening drew on, more and more Parisians had joined the army the Convention was collecting. As they heard about the growing strength of the opposition army, the sansculottes in front of City Hall began to waver. They were waiting for Robespierre to come and lead them, and when he didn't come, they grew frightened. One man slipped away, then another, then another. Then, at about midnight, an accident destroyed Robespierre's last hope of victory. Suddenly a thunderstorm struck Paris. The rain poured down in torrents and those sansculottes who were still waiting in front of the City Hall seized the excuse to make off. Within a few minutes, the square was empty. Even the soldiers who had rescued Hanriot had disappeared.

Meanwhile, inside the City Hall, Robespierre and a few advisers were arguing over what they should do. St. Just was there, and Hanriot, and Augustin Robespierre, the tyrant's brother, and Couthon, in his wheelchair. At about one o'clock, Robespierre finally decided to sign an appeal to the people of Paris to rise up in arms against the Convention. But even as he made his decision, soldiers gathered by the Convention were entering the building, and just as Robespierre began to sign his name to the document, they burst into the room.

A shot rang out — no one knows who fired it. The bullet shattered Robespierre's jaw and he fell across the table, his blood spattering over his call to arms. Couthon, terrified, crawled out of his wheelchair to hide under a table. He was picked up and thrown down a staircase, where he lay unconscious. Augustin Robespierre hurled himself out of a window, fell into a courtyard below, and was crippled. Hanriot also threw himself, or perhaps he was hurled, out of a window. He fell into a pile of manure and lay there, in a drunken stupor, for several hours before he was found.

Now the end was fast approaching for Robespierre. From the City Hall he was taken back to the offices of the Committee of Public Safety in the Tuileries Palace. There, in the very room where he had signed the orders that ruled France, he lay helpless on a table with a box of ammunition stuck under his head to prop it up. His shoes had dropped off. His bloodstained shirt hung open across his breast, his elegant pale blue coat was torn, and his stockings dropped about his ankles. While he lay, in agony from the pain of his shattered jaw, a mob of sightseers came to look down on him. Some taunted him mockingly. "Sire," said one, "Your Majesty seems to be suffering. What! Have you lost the power of speech?"

And these were the people, the ordinary men and women of Paris who, or so Robespierre had believed, adored him almost as if he were a god. Certainly there were tens of thousands of Parisians who had loved him; but they did not love him enough to take any more risks. Like the deputies in the Convention, most of the sansculottes were only ready to support the winning side. When Danton ruled France, they had acclaimed him as a hero. When he went to his death, they had watched him in silence. Now Robespierre was suffering the same fate.

It was the same at the Revolutionary Tribunal where

Robespierre and some twenty of his supporters were taken next day to be tried as enemies of the people. All through the previous day, while the struggle was raging in the Convention, the Tribunal had kept on with its grisly work. Late in the afternoon, police had come to arrest Dumas, the presiding judge. But when he was led away, another judge calmly took his place and the Tribunal worked on, even though the judges knew that Dumas would soon come before them as a "traitor."

During the day, some forty people had been condemned to death. Hearing of the events in the Convention, Sanson, the executioner, had suggested to Fouquier-Tinville that perhaps the executions should be delayed.

"No," Fouquier-Tinville had answered. "Justice must take its course. Do your work." And the condemned men and women had gone to the guillotine.

That crazy, implacable justice was indeed taking its course. The same judges and jurors who had obeyed Robespierre's every wish were now to have the job of condemning him as a traitor. Fouquier-Tinville knew that he himself would probably also be brought before the Tribunal as a "traitor." But he was obliged to sit in the courtroom in order to identify his master as "the conspirator, Robespierre." Because of his shattered jaw, Robespierre could not speak in his own defense. But even if he had been physically able to speak, he would not have been given the chance. Under the law which he himself had forced the Convention to pass, he was not allowed to defend himself, and the men whom he had named as judges condemned him and his supporters to death.

The Convention had decided that the people of Paris should be given the opportunity to watch the distinguished victims as they rode to their death. It therefore ordered the guillotine to be carried back and set up in its old position near the center of the city, in the Place de la Revolution. Huddled in their carts, Robespierre and his fellow terrorists rode along the same route which had been taken by Louis the Sixteenth, by the Girondins, by Marie Antoinette and by Danton. And, on their way, they passed the house where Robespierre had lived and where Danton had looked up to shout his famous prophecy: "Vile Robespierre. You will follow me."

Yet even Danton could not have anticipated the horrible humiliation of his murderers as they followed him to the scaffold. He at least had gone to his death standing firm and upright, his great head raised proudly as he gazed in contempt at the watching crowds. Robespierre rode crouched on a plank, still in agony from his shattered jaw. In the cart ahead, his brother Augustin, and Hanriot, both half dead, lay on the floor. And in the cart behind, the terrorist Couthon also lay sprawled out on the floor, trampled underfoot by his companions.

The people who had crowded the streets to see Danton go to the guillotine had watched him in silence. There was no such silence for Robespierre. Of all the crowds that had gathered to see "enemies of the Revolution" carried to their death, none had been as happy as this one. The Terror would end. The tyrant was about to die. Now the mass of Parisians who had remained quiet out of fear could show Robespierre what they really thought of him. Groups of people hung from windows along the route, laughing and cheering. Other groups gathered in the streets as the procession went by and danced for joy. And one woman spoke for millions of her country men and women when she burst through the guards around the carts and shouted out:

"Monster, I am drunk with joy to see you suffer. You are going to hell with the curses of all wives and mothers following you."

Around the guillotine, a huge mob stretched away, filling every inch of space in the great square. The guillotine fell and fell, and fell again. But of the twenty-two heads that dropped into the basket, only three were picked out and held up for the crowd to see. They were the heads of Robespierre, of Dumas and of Hanriot; the heads of the tyrant, and of the judge and of the soldier who had supported him. To the crowd, the sight of those heads spelled out the words: "The Terror is over." As each head was shown, it was greeted with a thunderous roar of joy, relief, and revenge.

The crowd, as it turned out, was wiser than the politicians. The conspirators who had plotted to send Robespierre and his friends to the guillotine had had no intention of bringing the Terror to an end. They had condemned Robespierre simply to save themselves, and they planned to have everything continue as it had before, except that now they, and not Robespierre, would be in control of France. Very soon, however, the conspirators found that they had started a process they could not stop. Except for a few fanatical Jacobins, the people of France were utterly sick of bloodshed and fear and suspicion; of the secret police, and the executions, and the never-ending stories about conspirators. Their desire to be free of it all was like a mighty flood. Robespierre had been the dyke that had held it back and, with his fall, the dyke collapsed.

Abruptly the Terror came to an end. In the prisons of Paris, thousands of men and women waited for the fatal roll call that would decide their fate. But the daily roll call had ended and was never to be heard again. Soon the Convention ordered that all political prisoners should be released, and thousands of people who had given up all hope found that they were free.

It was the same all over France. The prisons were emptied. The theaters, the restaurants, and the dance halls were reopened. The red cap of liberty, which had been the symbol of patriotism, was outlawed. Once again, the people of France were able to say what they wished and to walk the streets without fear. Instead, it was the men who had inflicted the fear who now had cause to be afraid. All over France, Jacobin leaders were driven out of the local governments. The Jacobin clubs were closed. The Revolutionary Tribunal was disbanded. The arch executioner, Fouquier-Tinville, followed his master to the guillotine. The Committee of Public Safety was deprived of its dictatorial powers, and gradually its members were replaced as the Convention established itself as the ruling government of France.

That fateful day of July 26, 1794, really marked the end of the French Revolution. It is true that the fall of Robespierre did not end the dreadful struggles that had kept France for five long years in a state of chaos and agony. There were to be more years of political battles and intrigues, of riots in the streets, even of civil war before the people could once again go about their daily work in peace. But the last of the great revolutionary leaders had passed from the scene, and, with his death, the period of the worst upheavals was over.

The French Revolution, however, was much more important than any of its leaders. More important than any of their quarrels. More important than the wars it had produced or its military victories and defeats. The effects of the Revolution have lasted till the present day. For the Revolu-

tion destroyed the old, unfair system in which a few rich
aristocrats ruled France while the mass of the people lived in
poverty. The Revolution proved that ordinary men and
women could rise up against tyrannical rulers. It proved
that every individual could enjoy the right to vote and be
treated equally under the law. It enabled the peasants to own
their own plots of land instead of having to work, like slaves,
for the rich landowners. It gave the working men and women
of the cities a new feeling of self-respect. It turned France
into a democracy.

From France, these principles spread out all over western
Europe. Other people followed the lead of the French revolutionaries. They, too, rose up against the kings and the aristocrats who ruled over them and asserted their own right to
share in the government. Few episodes in history have been
as horrible as the French Revolution. But few have done
more to improve the everyday lives of ordinary men and
women. Many of the leading revolutionaries were butchers
and liars, intriguers and cowards. As individuals, many, perhaps most, were despicable human beings. Yet through their
actions and their example, they helped hundreds of millions
of people who came after them to win the right to elect their
leaders : and so to live in freedom.

# INDEX